Avul Pakir Jainulabdeen Abdul Kalam was the eleventh President of India, from 2002 to 2007. He was a recipient of the Padma Bhushan, the Padma Vibhushan and the nation's highest civilian award, the Bharat Ratna.

Born in 1931 in Rameswaram in Tamil Nadu, Dr Kalam studied aeronautical engineering at the Madras Institute of Technology. He played a key role in the development of India's first satellite launch vehicle, the SLV-3; in the building and operationalization of India's strategic missile systems; and in the 1998 nuclear tests.

As an elder statesman, he was in the public eye for his role in offering counsel, reaching out to people and building bridges across religious and social divides. Dr Kalam's focus was ever on transforming India into a developed nation by 2020 and to this end he continued to travel across the country for his teaching assignments at IITs and IIMs, to address conferences and to meet students and people from all walks of life.

He passed away at one such lecture he had gone to deliver at Shillong on 27 July 2015. His message and influence continue to resonate with people across the country, and in all walks of life.

Srijan Pal Singh is a gold medallist MBA holder from the Indian Institute of Management, Ahmedabad, and has worked with the Boston Consulting Group. He is a social entrepreneur who has been involved in studying and evolving sustainable development systems with a thrust on rural areas. From 2009 to 2015, he also worked as an advisor and officer on special duty to Dr A.P.J. Abdul Kalam on promoting the concepts of energy independence and Providing Urban Amenities in Rural Areas (PURA), and co-authored with him two books: *Target 3 Billion* (2011) and *Reignited* (2015). He was named as one of the Global Leaders of Tomorrow by the St Gallen Leadership Symposium in Switzerland in 2014. He has also co-authored *Smart and Human* (2015) with G.R.K. Reddy.

ADVANTAGE INDIA

From Challenge to Opportunity

A.P.J. Abdul Kalam

and

Srijan Pal Singh

HarperCollins *Publishers* India

First published in India in 2015 by
HarperCollins *Publishers* India

Copyright © A.P.J. Abdul Kalam and Srijan Pal Singh 2015

P-ISBN: 978-93-5177-645-1
E-ISBN: 978-93-5177-646-8

2 4 6 8 10 9 7 5 3 1

A.P.J. Abdul Kalam and Srijan Pal Singh assert the moral right to be
identified as the authors of this work.

The views and opinions expressed in this book are the authors' own
and the facts are as reported by them, and the publishers
are not in any way liable for the same.

HarperCollins *Publishers*
A-75, Sector 57, Noida 201301, India
1 London Bridge Street, London, SE1 9GF, United Kingdom
Hazelton Lanes, 55 Avenue Road, Suite 2900, Toronto, Ontario M5R 3L2
and 1995 Markham Road, Scarborough, Ontario M1B 5M8, Canada
25 Ryde Road, Pymble, Sydney, NSW 2073, Australia
195 Broadway, New York, NY 10007, USA

Typeset in 11/14 Electra LT Regular at
SÜRYA

Printed and bound at
Thomson Press (India) Ltd.

This book is dedicated to the ever-lasting memory of Dr A.P.J. Abdul Kalam (1931–2015), who, through his life, gave us the confidence to believe that 'I can do it, we can do it and India will do it'.

—Srijan Pal Singh

CONTENTS

ACKNOWLEDGEMENTS

In writing this book, our thoughts and ideas have evolved through two decades of experience and interaction with various stakeholders, including government functionaries, manufacturing industries, bureaucracy, environmentalists, social and spiritual leaders, educationists, healthcare institutes, many local business units and a general audience aspiring to contribute in their own ways to the nation and their families. A large portion of the thoughts expressed in this book are essentially extensions of contemplations, anxieties, dreams, perils, ambitions, hopes and challenges of all these citizens revolving around the fundamental need of the nation to identify and harness the advantages of India. We thank all these stakeholders, friends, acquaintances, some even strangers and the young community, who have openly shared their views and thoughts which have taken the shape of a coherent theory and examples in this book. We sincerely hope that our book captures their ingenious thoughts.

We also express our acknowledgement and gratitude to Shri Harry Sheridon, Shri R.K. Prasad and Shri Dhanshyam Sharma for their regular help towards putting this book together. We also extend our thanks to Shri G.R.K. Reddy, Mr G.S. Naveen Kumar, Professor Basav Roychoudhury (IIM Shillong), Mr Saurav and Mr Jayraj Pandya, who helped research and compile data for this book.

We also sincerely acknowledge the contribution of Mr Krishan Chopra of HarperCollins along with that of Ms Iti Khurana,

Mr Sameer Mahale, Mr Siddhesh Inamdar, Mr Rajinder Ganju and Ms Bonita Vaz-Shimray for their excellent support in publishing this book in record time.

PROLOGUE

THE IDEATION WALK

Location:
10 Rajaji Marg, New Delhi, a few months ago

Participants:
Dr A.P.J. Abdul Kalam: APJ
Srijan Pal Singh: SPS

Srijan: Good morning! As we begin to write this book today on creating an India with a competitive advantage, I am curious to know how you see this book. Where does this lead to?

APJ: It is not just a book. I think we are trying to make a blueprint for the nation's development up to 2020. You see, the nation is going through a change—at an ever-increasing rate. We are trying to assess this change, find the points at which the people and the government need to intervene to help us achieve our aim of an economically developed India by 2020. And this has to be the mission of every Indian, wired into the conscience and work of every person no matter where, in schools, in colleges, in offices, in courtrooms and in Parliament.

SPS: Yes indeed. Let us make this book a personal mission for every Indian. A script of how individual actions, small steps, can be aggregated into a great journey. But I have a doubt. I wonder how is such an endeavour possible.

1

APJ: India is a vast nation with many different challenges. Moreover, the issues and opportunities of one region are different from that in another. A Bihar is very different from a Kerala or from a J&K. This makes single-agenda missions difficult. But then, I remember what my guru, Satish Dhawan, once said: 'If you undertake difficult missions, there will be many problems. Never let the problems become your captain. You become the captain of the problems, defeat them and succeed.'

SPS: Indeed. In the past one year there has been many a significant shift in the nation—beginning with the change of government itself. Many state governments have also changed. New policies, goals and dreams are being pursued and there is a fresh urgency towards them. What are the changes you see and where is India heading?

APJ: I think there has been a realignment of energies for new missions while also continuation of existing missions. The nation has entered the last five years before it sees 2020, and there is an urgency to achieve the status of a developed India without poverty across the spectrum.

SPS: That is why we need to focus on a multi-pronged approach across many sectors concurrently. What do you think is our position in this respect?

APJ: Yes, we need to go into mission mode now. Set a target, and see who all, which all departments and initiatives can work together towards it. It would be good to make mission teams which can bring together system thinking, system design and system integration.

SPS: Let me get to some specific missions which are the pillars of development for India today and which we will be covering in this book. What do you think about the Make in India campaign? Many people are sceptical about it for a variety of reasons, including on grounds of attitude, education and infrastructure. You have led in the indigenous development of missiles, satellites and many other landmark projects. Do you see significant impediments to a large-scale mission of Make in India?

APJ: Well, let us be clear on this. Make in India is quite ambitious. But we need such high aspirations. India used to be a global hub of goods before the British destroyed the competency of our industries. So, I believe Indians have always had it in them to be global manufacturers. Education . . . yes we do need to look at the pyramid below the IITs and IIMs—much needs to be done to make the workforce competitive. I agree with the infrastructure concern. India has seen an unbalanced infra growth—variations are rampant across states and sectors. For instance, while the telecom and internet sectors have made remarkable progress, many villages still are not connected with roads and power. Physical infrastructure cannot be ignored for manufacturing growth.

Also, we need to ensure that we do not become the low-cost, low-value assembly line of the world. If we go on that path, the growth will come at a great price and pain to the people. We have the ideas of the youth, the wisdom of the ages and the vibrancy of a democracy. With these three forces, we need to do original research to design, develop and manufacture in India.

SPS: Right. I get that. What about Digital India? There is a very promising plan to connect villages, schools and the base of the pyramid with digital connectivity. India has seen its service sector growth led by such an internet revolution in its cities.

APJ: Yes, Digital India has the potential to activate the knowledge connectivity needed in villages and remote areas. We need to bridge the gaps of lower level of literacy, language and customized content, though.

SPS: I think Digital India is a mission with tremendous potential for collateral benefits. Imagine a comprehensive data of all records that are interlinked to each other for all citizens. It would create a wonderful tool for data analysis, alerts and actions. It would also go a long way in addressing the issue of corruption. Speaking of corruption, what do you think is the solution to it? I have seen a lot of young people asking you this question.

APJ: It has to be a movement beginning in the homes, spreading to schools and working towards educating the new generation and giving a new meaning to citizenship. To win against corruption we need system thinking, and that begins at home.

SPS: What kind of citizenship are we talking about?

APJ: Let me see. Do you remember the sudden stop we made at the dhaba in Azamgarh?

SPS: Yes, of course! On our way to the Varanasi airport.

APJ: Tell me, as a management graduate, what did you observe?

SPS: I think for a small dhaba, with its limited resources, it was a workstation of great efficiency. I remember, the shop owner with a single help made fresh tea, warmed the snacks, served the food for all of us including the security personnel and then acted as the cleaner and cashier too.

APJ: Yes, that is right. Also, did you notice the smile with which he did all this?

SPS: Yes.

APJ: That smile comes from the intense spirit of service which the man harboured. He took pride in his little shop, kept it clean. Taking pride in one's duty is the key to ethical professionalism.

SPS: When one cherishes the outcome, one enjoys the walk, even if it is a difficult one. And such people, who take pride in their duty, always outshine the mediocre through their results, don't they?

APJ: Yes. Then they become examples of 'Work with Integrity and Succeed with Integrity.'

SPS: Specific to the issues surrounding corruption, I often hear people say that corruption is unavoidable and honesty is akin to foolishness. It is sad to know that from the notion of 'The honest always stand alone' we have now moved to a point that 'The honest will not be allowed to survive at all.'

APJ: It is true that corruption is becoming an acceptable social phenomenon in the last past few years. We need a comprehensive, multi-dimensional reform which can strike at the roots of corruption.

SPS: But where does it all start? What is the origin of corruption?

APJ: I believe corruption comes from lack of purpose. A goalless mind is easily swayed by short-term materialistic pleasures. That is the origin of corruption. It can gnaw away like a termite at one's conscience.

SPS: But sometimes we do have a purpose and never act on it.

APJ: True. Most people have a definite purpose. Most of the time they even know of it, but then they do little to act on it. Author Napoleon Hill talks of this in *Outwitting the Devil* when he says, '. . . Everyone is born with the privilege of being definite, but 98 out of 100 people lose that privilege by sleeping over it.' This is so true.

SPS: Another aspect which makes people deviate from the path of morality is fear. The fear of losing comforts and materials which they feel they need to be happy.

APJ: Fear and indecision of purpose go hand in hand. If you are inspired by a great mission, all your happiness and excitement in life will come from that purpose. It is like the North Star which guides all ships. Only when there is the dark cloud of indecision over the North Star of purpose does one look for the little candles of worldly materials to find happiness in life.

SPS: I am glad you raised the issue of indecision. Corruption seems to be a psychological ailment of being unable to decide. It is when people are unable to find their way in ambiguous situations that they sway into immorality. Our education system needs to be geared to help citizens cope with the difficult choices between identity versus integrity, price versus pride and loyalty versus morality. Only then will they be able to decide ethically and be willing to forgo potential short-term comforts for long-term satisfaction in life.

APJ: Yes. Education is the cornerstone of our fight for a morally upright society. Only enlightened citizens can carry forward the torch of ethical living. We need people of courage, who keep daring on the path of integrity because they have an unflinching belief in their purpose. They may stumble and fall at times, but then they get up, they try different paths, but their purpose and goals never change. India needs such citizens. We need to strive for such a colossal change.

SPS: Let us get going with this book, this mission then, sir.

APJ: Sure. Let us begin.

1

THE UNSEEN ADVANTAGES

In July 2014, both of us visited Jaunpur district in Uttar Pradesh to attend the National Children's Science Congress. July is a hot month in this eastern Uttar Pradesh district—and because of the dry weather and gusts of wind, the loose soil is blown across the countryside. Such a local weather phenomenon can occur frequently throughout the day and obscure the view and keep the air dusty.

On the evening prior to the function, we took a flight from Delhi, the city which is now home to both of us, and travelled to Allahabad. Allahabad, the holy site where Ganga and Yamuna meet, is the closest airport to Jaunpur. The morning required us to still cover about 120 kilometres from the guest house to the Jaunpur venue in an interior school ground. Needing to reach at 12.30 p.m., and forewarned of some bad patches of road by our Delhi office, we started off at 9.30 a.m.—resolute to make it on time for the event where a few thousand enthusiastic students had assembled from all over the country.

We began our journey on the national highway. About two hours later, our convoy of five cars and a mid-sized van started moving onto narrower and narrower roads. Soon we hit an area where the combined effect of moving tyres on broken roads and local winds on parched soil engulfed us in a thick cover of dust. We kept on moving into this dust—our only guide being the car ahead of us, whose

7

driver cleverly turned on its tail lights to help us follow it better.
The clouds of fine dust obscured our view of the huts, animals and
trees along the road. Seeing this dust, I asked Srijan, 'Are we on a
road or have we lost our way on some kuccha (mud) pathway?' He
pulled out his mobile phone and switched on the GPS mode. To
the surprise of all of us, amidst all this dust, the cell phone could
still manage high-speed internet of the third generation (3G)
network. On Google Maps a blue moving dot indicated our
position—all along we were moving on the state highway—
supposedly a rapid movement road. The third generation mobile
network was a theoretical four-lane road. All along our journey
henceforth, in dust or no dust, our mobile GPS kept a continuous
track of our route: it became our 'periscope' in the sea of dust.

Another one hour passed like this. Significantly slowed down by
the road's condition and visibility, we were fighting a losing battle
against time. Then we hit a stop. Our driver told us there was a
railway crossing which was closed and we would have to wait for
five minutes. Of course, we had little choice.

But as the tyres stopped rolling the dust settled around us—and
for once we got a clear view of the outside. A shop board nearby
told us the name of the area—Badshahpur, or the land of the king.

Going by our description of the road, one might think that
calling the place a king's place is ironic. But that is not the case.
The settling dust showed three different scenes that were like a
revelation of the potential of Badshahpur.

First, we saw hoardings atop nearby shops wooing customers to
use mobile money transfer via M-Pesa, a product started in Kenya
by an NGO and then taken over by the multinational Vodafone,
and Airtel Money, an Indian-grown multinational. The two vied
for advertising space in the market near the railway crossing. We
later learnt that migrant workers in Delhi and Mumbai from the
region frequently use mobile money transfer to send money back
home. Half of those receiving the money can barely read the dial
pad on their phone, but nearly all are able to manage the transaction

seamlessly. The pressing necessity for rapid money transfer has enabled them to invent and skip the stage of basic literacy and land straight into digital literacy (or an even fancier term, 'm-literacy'— mobile literacy).

Second, slightly at a distance, we glimpsed a couple of training centres on the first floor of a building. The signboards read, 'Maruti Computer Training Centre' and 'Sai Mobile Repairing Centre'.

Named after two important spiritual symbols of Indian society, one from the Vedic period and another only about one hundred years old, these two skill development centres were symbolic of how remote areas of the nation are abreast with the most advanced technological consumer tools of the modern era.

But there is more to the story of these two centres. Below each signboard, they listed a set of diploma courses being offered and then the line, 'Courses in Hindi, English and Bhojpuri', followed by 'Special 20% discount for girls'. That is how India has been striving to blend local languages with global knowledge needs and how it has taken an initiative to include its 50% women population as a potent economic entity. We could not help but smile at Badshahpur's benevolence in the way it included people of all languages and genders. Was it not a true mark of a king's land?

Then the third sight came. Soon an electric train whizzed past us. Powered by 10,000 volts of continuous supply, it represented the reach and reliability of the Indian railways, one of the oldest and largest railway systems in the world. Perhaps, all through our journey on dusty roads we travelled past many of the thousands of villages in India which still have little or no access to power. The rumbling diesel sets in some of the shops nearby also told that power quality was still an issue even in the marketplace. The massive uncoordinated mesh of wires descending from the electric pole made us doubtful that this may be a case of 'line losses', or unaccounted and non-revenue generating leakage of power, due to pilferage or poor hardware. In large parts of the country, such leakages may be up to 40% of the total power supplied. Yet, metres

away India is still able to guarantee 24x7 power to the railway
locomotive. This made us wonder, is the case of people still waiting
for power to arrive in their villages more an issue of lack of generation
and resources or lack of management of the resources we already
have?

*

To our disappointment, we reached the Children's Science
Congress about half an hour late, but the organizers had recalibrated
the programme so that there was no waiting time for the children.
Indians are among the best in the world at managing delays and
unforeseen events—as a Western friend once told us, 'Indians
know best how to ride the horse of chaos.' We are still wondering
whether that was a compliment.

As the day passed we had another destination to reach. Our
flight back was scheduled from the holy city of Benares (Varanasi)
and in the middle we had a short function at a hospital to attend in
Azamgarh. Azamgarh is almost at midpoint between Jaunpur and
Varanasi, so it was only a little diversion for us.

All along the highway we noticed a number of small shops
huddled together selling tea, snacks and clothes. Occasionally
there was an air-conditioned restaurant, electronic store and pharma
shop. Together, in their diversity and balance of commodities, they
represented 'horizontal supermarkets'—there was hardly anything
one could not find in these stretches of shops. There was no shop
plan, no dedicated corridors or floors—the entire planning was
organic and automatic.

We were enticed to experience these rural commercial spaces.
So, in the middle of our journey, we requested for a stop and
entered a small tea stall. Behind a glass display screen some of the
choicest Indian snacks were displayed—samosas and pakoras, and
for the sweeter toothed, jalebis and barfis. At the counter was a
refrigerator stacked with international branded colas jostling for
space with a locally made tangy drink called 'Banta' (basically

carbonated lime juice with rock salt and sugar). Looking at a large convoy with many policemen, the shopowner quickly came out from his place behind the counter and laid a few plastic chairs along a small table. He told us his name was Kuber—named after the divine custodian of wealth. We asked him, 'What is good to eat today?' Kuber had an air of confidence when he replied, 'Everything here is fresh, replaced twice a day.' Then he added, 'I am a specialist in tea flavours.' Encouraged, we asked him what did he mean by 'specialist in tea', to which he gave a listing, wrapped neatly in clear polythene, which read 'Tea Menu'. In that menu, he had listed at least a dozen different flavours—including ginger, lemon, chocolate, pudina (mint), Darjeeling and many other variants of tea. It was surprising to see a little shop in an obscure highway filled with such imagination and innovation. We quickly ordered about a dozen cups of tea for all of us along with some samosas. Immediately Kuber and his one helper washed the utensils and went about their work with the utmost hygiene. In five minutes all our requests were laid on the table. It was one of the most refreshing teas we've had—all by an entrepreneur in Azamgarh. While we were having the tea, Kuber told us that he lived not far from the stall, that the helper was actually his nephew, that he had two daughters, both of whom went to school, and that business was generally good.

We had a few takeaways besides the tea.

First, it showed how local markets create entrepreneurs. India is filled with consumers with reasonable purchasing power. A single road, even in Azamgarh, has enough 'GDP' to support these entrepreneurs.

Second, these entrepreneurs generate the value of innovation. Kuber told us how he spent many days studying the different varieties of tea, customized it according to local tastes, and then went all the way to the district headquarters to get his menu altered and printed many times.

Third, enterprise can be in a local context. While we have nothing against large food chains, and they have their own value, the producers in these regional pockets can find spaces with these entrepreneurs who are catering to the local market. It is a delicate demand-production-supply balance which needs to be handled carefully. Kuber's fridge with Banta and Cola together was a testimony to how domestic, sometimes even regional brands, can challenge global and celebrity-endorsed brands.

The experience raised some questions in our minds, which became the basis of our chai discussion in Kuber's shop.

What can be done to promote such in-house brands that serve as the backbone of local economies?

How do high-speed mobile connections run seamlessly where roads barely exist?

What makes mobile money prosper where poverty alleviation flounders?

What enables 10,000 volts to run uninterrupted trains when 220 volts is still a technical challenge?

What makes the Kubers of our villages think big but yet keeps them away from basic education?

Is India a land of dismal challenges that weigh it down by their scale or is it a land of magnificent opportunities?

India is witnessing a new thrust in policy and planning since 2014. As a run-up to the landmark year of 2020, the parliament and people have endorsed many new missions like Make in India, skill development of the youth, hygiene and health for the nation, smart cities, Digital India, new energy policies and new rural development models.

Rather than look into a distant future, we consider what are the opportunities for the nation for the next four to five years. What are the key challenges to address? And how can we learn from our own experiences and from the lessons of other nations so as to leapfrog them?

Further in this book we dive into the history of India and also go into some statistical depth to gauge India's future path, showing its competitive advantages and disadvantages. We will make an attempt to blend one author's professional experience of more than seven decades in multiple roles in the government, including as President, with the freshness of ideas of the Generation X of the other author.

2

FROM FALLEN HERO
TO RISING STAR

THE FORGOTTEN PEOPLE

It was the most tumultuous and chaotic period in mankind's history. The Second World War was raging across Europe, Asia and the far Pacific. By 1943, the war had already consumed many nations, claiming the lives of large numbers of soldiers and civilians. 'History's biggest genocide' is what the media called it.

In the same period, a significantly large and yet silent theatre of death was operating in Bengal, right under the nose of the British rule. The Bengal Famine was the outcome of the callousness of an empire and would rank as one of the worst disasters of our times. Yet few history books would ever talk about it. It took Hitler a decade, starting from the mid-1930s to kill six million Jews, gypsies and other communities under the 'extermination list' of the Nazis. But it took only one year, 1943, for British policies to accomplish the mass murder of four million Indians by condemning them to a slow death from hunger, disease and sometimes by their own hand as they were driven to desperation.

It would be not wrong to call the Bengal Famine a 'manmade disaster' arising out of Churchill's policies which were directly responsible for the hunger and the disaster. It is on record that Bengal had a bountiful harvest in 1942, but the British started diverting vast quantities of food grain from India to Britain, to supply their war efforts, contributing to a massive food shortage in the areas comprising present-day West Bengal, Odisha, Bihar and Bangladesh.[1]

Author Madhusree Mukerjee writes in her book, *Churchill's Secret War*: 'Parents dumped their starving children into rivers and wells. Many took their lives by throwing themselves in front of trains. Starving people begged for the starchy water in which rice had been boiled. Children ate leaves and vines, yam stems and grass. People were too weak even to cremate their loved ones.'

It was a humiliation for Bengal, which was considered the richest and most prosperous region in the world by the father of political economics, Adam Smith, in his book *The Wealth of Nations*, in 1776. Subhas Chandra Bose, who was fighting against the British through his Azad Hind Fauj, offered to send rice from Myanmar (Burma), but the British media censors did not even allow his offer to be reported. Even when the Indian leaders and the viceroy, Lord Wavell, pleaded with London to release food from the reserves which the British already had, there was no action. To all the messages and telegrams, Churchill's only reply was, 'So why hasn't Gandhi died yet?' He would tell his Secretary of State for India, Leopold Amery, 'I hate Indians. They are a beastly people with a beastly religion.' The famine was their own fault, he declared at a war-cabinet meeting, for 'breeding like rabbits'.[2]

Churchill's attitude, though genocidal and horribly racist, was not unique. The British Raj was all about exploitation anyway. During the British rule in India, from 1765 to 1947, there were approximately 25 major famines spread through states such as Tamil Nadu in south India, Bihar in the north, and Bengal in the east; altogether, between 50 and 80 million Indians were the victims of famines.

Period	Annual GDP growth rate
Colonial India (1900-1947)	0.9%
1950s (1950-60)	3.7%
1960s	3.4%
1970s	3.4%
1980s	5.2%
1990s	5.9%
2000s	7.6%

TABLE 1: GDP growth over the years

In 1700 CE, just before the East India Company established control, India's share of the world income stood at 27%. In 1947, when they left, India's share in world income was less than 3%. Colonial India had a GDP growth rate of less than 1%. As soon as the British left, despite the difficulties of a new and painfully divided nation, the GDP growth rate stood at 3.7%. Independent India never saw a single major famine. The newly born India inherited a lagging agriculture system from the British. Moreover, with Pakistan being carved in both West and East, India also lost some of its most fertile lands used for wheat in Punjab and rice in Bengal. In 1950, with one mildly bad harvest season, India was on the brink of its first famine as an independent nation. At 50.82 million tonnes and 357 million people to feed, Prime Minister Nehru, through his sister and the envoy to the United States, Vijayalakshmi Pandit, sent a formal request for a wheat aid of 2 million tonnes to the US government.

While President Truman was in favour of it, the Indian request faced stiff resistance from the Senate and Congress, in part due to high-handedness and also due to sheer ignorance about India. In the end, Nehru had to revise his request: India would now take the wheat as a loan of $190 million and not as an aid. It would be July 1951 when the deal was finally signed. Nehru would aggregate the pain of the world's largest democracy, 'We would be unworthy of the high responsibilities with which we have been charged if we bartered our country's self-respect or freedom of action, even for something we need badly.'[3]

In 1954, Dwight Eisenhower, successor to Truman, signed the Agricultural Trade Development and Assistance Act—or Public Law (PL) 480. PL 480 would become, on the surface, the basis of food assistance by the US to other nations, and behind the scenes, the instrument of arm-twisting food-deficit nations into diplomatic submission. PL 480 allowed food-deficient countries to pay for American food imports in their own currencies instead of in US dollars. Nations whose currency was suffering due to economic instability were its target segment. India became both the largest beneficiary and gravest victim of PL 480. PL 480 would be a household name in Indian homes for the next two decades.

Two factors made India reliant on PL 480. First, India faced almost a perennial food shortage in those days due to poor productivity. Second, the Indian rupee was depreciating, falling from Rs 3.30 for a dollar in 1948, to around 4.70 in the 1950s and then suddenly slipping to Rs 7.50 a dollar in 1966. PL 480 allowed India to pay in rupees and not dollars, and hence bypass this currency devaluation problem. The dependency became so dominant that when an Indian official was asked by a news reporter about the adequacy of the country's grain stocks, he responded, 'Our reserves are in the grain elevators in Kansas (USA).'[4]

PL 480 wheat would arrive in ships from the US that was unloaded into flat-bottomed boats which took the grain up the Ganga river and its tributaries to reach parts of the country where the drought was most severe and the risk of starvation the greatest. Logistically, the supply was remarkably successful. But it broke the morale of the nation—as India was termed to be in a ship-to-mouth condition.[5]

At its peak in 1965, India had imported 10 million tonnes of wheat under PL 480.[6] This is when a series of events changed the food equation of India.

In 1965 India went into a costly war with Pakistan. Then around the same period, Prime Minister Lal Bahadur Shastri told an American journalist, in reply to a question, that the war and invasion of Vietnam 'was an act of aggression [by the United States]'.[7] Angered by this statement, President Lyndon Johnson decided to unleash the hidden agenda of PL 480.

He put India, now heavily reliant on the wheat, on a 'short-tether' policy. Now onwards, ships carrying food for India would often be diverted, usually at the last minute, to other destinations. Desperate at its empty grain coffers, the Indian government would then run from one country to another looking for food. Many told the US president that what the Indian PM had said about the Vietnam War was no different from what the UN Secretary-General and the Pope were saying. To this, Johnson retorted: 'The Pope and the Secretary-General do not need our wheat.'[8]

Independent India did not let famine strike it, but 1965 hurt its self-esteem. This is when the change began. Prime Minister Shastri inspired the whole nation, rich and poor, beginning with himself, to go on weekly fasts to save food for the have-nots. Till date many Indians continue the fast.

In the late 1960s, India also embarked on the Green Revolution and transformed its productivity. In 1966, under Food and Agriculture Minister C. Subramaniam, India took the bold step to import 18,000 tonnes of wheat seed from Mexico, and adapted the seed to Indian conditions under the guidance of Dr Norman Borlaug. This remains, till date, the largest import of seeds of any cereal crop in history.

As per an earlier demarcated programme, the government distributed the seed to farmers in Punjab and western Uttar Pradesh where irrigation was available. The results were promising. The very first wheat harvest after cultivating high-yielding seeds in 1967 was five tonnes more than the previous yield per acre. The Green Revolution had begun. From 50 million tonnes in 1950, India's foodgrain output went up to 74 million tonnes in 1967. This became 171 million tonnes in 1990, an increase of more than two and a half times.

India also improved distribution by establishing state-organized markets for better supply and prices. It gave highly subsidized food to the poor through the Public Distribution System—to date there are 400,000 such state-supported fair price shops, popularly called ration shops, across the nation.

Six decades after the Bengal Famine, in which wells were filled with hungry children, thrown by their own parents unable to see their slow death by starvation—in 2003–04, India guaranteed free cooked meals to every single child coming to school through the world's largest cooked meal distribution scheme.

Exactly seven decades after the Bengal Famine, for which Churchill blamed the Indians themselves, India finally gave the right to food to all its citizens and under the National Food Security Act 2013 essential food grains were guaranteed to nearly all. All this was funded by its own budget. The once enslaved 'beastly people', as termed by the British PM, had now built an economy thrice the size of that of their former master.[9] In the early 21st century, India's home-grown companies had acquired some of the largest British companies.

By no means are we saying that India has achieved an ideal state; in fact we have a long way to go. But it is important to give a perspective to India's transformation since independence. Today there are many across the world who regard India as a rising star.

One of the authors of this book was born sixteen years before independence and saw his education during the Raj period. The other author was seeing the year 2000 by the time he turned sixteen. The difference in the two Indias captures the value of being a free nation. As Prime Minister Jawaharlal Nehru said in his speech on the eve of India's Independence, towards midnight on 14 August 1947, 'We end today a period of ill fortunes and India discovers herself again . . . This is no time for petty and destructive criticism, no time for ill will or blaming others. We have to build the noble mansion of free India where all her children may dwell.'[10]
In this book we navigate India's missions of the future to reclaim its

glory, to harness its resources and to create the noble mansion of prosperity and growth the forefathers of the nation envisioned.

POLITICAL AND ECONOMIC INCLUSION

Any nation is essentially composed of two systems—its political system and its economic system. Often they come so close to each other that they become indistinguishable, but nevertheless they remain as two distinct systems, which see a cyclic period of cooperation and opposition.

The political system is the way a society chooses the rules which will govern it and the resources of the nation will be utilized.[11] The political system may vary from democratic to monarchial to theological.

The economic system is the way a society harnesses the resources, natural and human, for the generation of wealth. It decides how wealth is owned, trade laws, and the entrepreneurial environment in a nation, among other things.

Both political and economic institutions can either be inclusive or extractive.[12] Inclusive political systems broadly divide power across different levels and clearly define the boundaries for each level. They minimize the overlap, have a strong independent judiciary, free press and fair ways to measure the performance of those in power. Extractive political systems have uneven concentration of power at the top, weak judiciary and political patronage in economic entities. The winner succeeds on the basis of political proximity and crony capitalism flourishes. Corruption is hence rampant.

An inclusive economic system thrives on well-defined property laws of secured ownership. It allows every citizen, whether rich or poor, equality of opportunity, thereby motivating people to dream big. It allows them to pursue a variety of careers and offers education and social development of high quality at affordable prices. An extractive economic system, on the other hand, ends up making the rich even richer, and is based on commanding resources and then shaping policy in such a way that competition is eliminated.

Clearly, an extractive political system and extractive economic system are close allies and nurture each other.

Though we must concede this is not always true. There are examples when political systems which were extractive were able to generate economic systems which were inclusive and growth focused—and vice versa, when inclusive political systems could only yield extractive economic systems with strong concentration of wealth.

For instance, Singapore had a single prime minister, Lee Kuan Yew, from 1959 to 1990 who, though liberal in policy making, was also known for being unforgiving of his political opponents.[13]

President Park Chung-hee of South Korea (1962–1979) also was known for centralizing power. Park had promised after taking office for his second term in 1967 that in accordance with the 1963 constitution, which limited the president to two consecutive terms, he would step down in 1971. However, soon after his 1967 victory, he and his party successfully pushed through an amendment allowing the incumbent president—himself—to run for three consecutive terms. In 1971 he narrowly won another election. He then declared a state of emergency shortly after being sworn in 'based on the dangerous realities of the international situation'. In 1972, Park dissolved the legislature and suspended the constitution in a self-coup. A new constitution was drafted which gave him absolute powers. In many ways, both these leaders represent extractive political systems, but both Singapore and South Korea made rapid economic progress, which was inclusive, during these periods.

Similarly, Tunisia, in North Africa, saw its own version of economic and social progress with an extractive political system under President Habib Bourguiba, who ruled the nation from 1957 to 1987. While Bourguiba established a single-party state and a personality cult around him, calling himself 'Supreme Warrior', he is known as a reformist. According to an account, '. . . the Bourguiba government's reforms include female emancipation, public education, family planning, a modern, state-run healthcare system, a campaign to improve literacy, administrative, financial and economic organization', besides helping build the country's infrastructure.'

Of course, such examples are rare in history.

A primary role of an inclusive political system is to identify monopolies and ensure that they are eliminated under the rule of law. If monopolies are allowed to exist, they will surely start dictating policy—if a handful of men acquire enough power to dictate and control the government, they will surely do so. Such is the nature of monopolies.

★

Is India's political system inclusive?

Surely, it was bold enough to give a 12% literate population the right to select their government regardless of their caste, creed, gender, economic class or race. In this regard, it was perhaps the first amongst all major democracies to do so. For instance, the US, the oldest democracy in the world, was established in 1787. The right to vote was then given only to White males. It took almost a century after this for the US to extend voting rights to all races. And it took about 133 years, in 1920, for it to give women the right to vote.

During the first few elections in India, literacy was so low that most parties and their candidates relied more on symbols rather than names while wooing their voters. Even today, during elections, the streets are painted in many symbols, from hands, lotuses, elephants, cycles, cookers and almost anything which has a recall value and is sanctioned by the Election Commission. The Election Commission itself speaks for political inclusion in the system and has remained staunch to its task regardless of the government in power. Above all this, the Supreme Court remains one of the most independent courts in the world—and this freedom percolates down to the high courts and lower courts—though it does get more diluted as it trickles down.

But before we claim the Indian political system to be inclusive there is another story to consider. The political field is also becoming an expensive arena—unevenly skewed in favour of the very rich. The average value of the assets of a Lok Sabha MP is Rs 14.6 crore.[14] Eight-two per cent of the elected members of Parliament have assets of over Rs 1 crore. In 2009, this figure was 58% and in 2004 this figure stood at 30%. Further troubling is the fact that 34% of the MPs in 2014 face criminal charges, up from 30% and 24% in 2009 and 2004 respectively.[15] An average of sixteen candidates contested from each of the 541 constituencies in the 2014 Lok Sabha elections. And more than 60 lakh (6 million) citizens decided to 'dump' their vote by pressing the freshly inducted NOTA button (None of the Above), expressing thereby their view that they did not even find a single candidate worthy of their vote.

What about the Economic System? Are we having an inclusive system or an extractive one? Let us analyse this briefly with some data.

Table 2 shows India's relative position in the number of billionaires and millionaires (in dollar terms) and then compares its situation in the share of people below poverty line. India is positioned at 13th place for the number of millionaires—a rising upper-class segment. But this does not match with the India's ranking in the number of super-rich billionaires (over Rs 6000 crore)—India is ranked third in this list. Many of those in the list are first-generation entrepreneurs associated from the IT, real estate and manufacturing sectors. Hence, India, especially in the recent past, has done remarkably well in wealthy individuals. Several of them have been instrumental in creating employment opportunities in the nation.

Relative position in the number of millionaires (figure in bracket indicates the total number of millionaires)[16]	Relative position in the number of billionaires (figure in bracket indicates the total number of billionaires)[17]	Relative position in the percentage of population below poverty line (figure in bracket indicates the percentage of BPL)[18]
USA (5134)	USA (537)	Taiwan (1.5)
Japan (1587)	China (430)	China (6.1)
China (1432)	**India (97)**	Switzerland (7.6)
UK (411)	Russia (93)	France (7.9)
Germany (345)	UK (80)	Canada (9.4)
Switzerland (322)	Germany (72)	Russia (11)
Italy (270)	Switzerland (60)	Germany (15.5)
Taiwan (246)	Brazil (56)	USA (15.1)
Hong Kong (212)	Chinese Taipei-Taiwan (48)	Japan (16)
France (200)	France (46)	South Korea (16)
Singapore (188)	Japan (45)	UK (16.2)
Canada (185)	Canada (39)	Brazil (21.4)
India (162)	South Korea (33)	**India (29.8)**

TABLE 2: The rich–poor divide in India

But there is a flip side to this story which is highlighted in the third column of the table. Our worry stems from the column showing the percentage of people below the poverty line. Compared to its peers in the list of wealthy individuals, India is not only at the bottom in this list, but at almost one-third, it also way higher than the rest. This reflects a trend to leave a huge number out of economic progress and struggling for basic amenities. Eighty per cent of these Below Poverty Line people reside in India's 600,000 villages, often languishing away from the glare of popular attention. We believe this is a challenge we need to address and solve in order to make our economy truly inclusive and we will be discussing this aspect in later chapters.

3

PATHWAYS TO NATIONAL PRODUCTIVITY

TWO EXPERIENCES FROM AGNI ON HOW TO MAKE IN INDIA

The 1980s saw a series of geo-political shifts and manoeuvrings. The world barely had come out of the two oil shocks of the mid and late 1970s, when the Arab nations banned oil supplies to the US in 1973 and then in 1979 the stand-off between the US and Iran saw oil prices spike to unprecedented heights. Throughout the 1980s, the US had a trust deficit in almost entire Asia. At the same time, the Soviet Union was seen as a giant bear on the descent. Towards the latter half of the decade, Mikhail Gorbachev took command of the ailing Soviet economy—he would eventually fail to hold the nation together; in his defence, there was very little he could do. In 1989, the world turned on its head with the fall of the Berlin Wall, with media airing shots of thousands of East and West Germans inching up the wall of separation—uniting the two nations once more. In these times, global alliances were quickly being reconfigured to prepare for the unimaginable and yet inevitable fall of the mighty Soviet Union and the rise of a new world order.

As we said earlier, the mistrust of the US with almost everyone who was not a part of NATO was at its peak in these times. Hence, the 1980s was a period of strained relations between India and the

US. Despite India being the largest democracy, the US government perceived India as ideologically closer to the Soviet Union. India on its own part was still having fresh memories of the US sending its nuclear aircraft carrier, USS *Enterprise*, into the Bay of Bengal when India and Pakistan were in the middle of the 1971 war. The US also tried to push resolutions in the United Nations favouring Pakistan and asking for an immediate cease fire, while the Indian army was driving deep into Bangladesh. These were vetoed by the Soviet Union. This had added to the woes of 1965, when the US had deployed its short-tether policy, exploiting India's dependence on PL 480 for diplomatic pressure, as we discussed earlier. The scars had not fully healed in the next one decade.

In India, the late 1980s was an exciting time if you were working in the defence sector. The research thrust given by Prime Minister Indira Gandhi a half decade earlier was now yielding results. The Defence Research and Development Laboratory (DRDL) was working overtime on indigenous missiles, tanks and other hi-tech hardware. The sector was still fledgling, but nevertheless working hard to grow giant wings. This also meant we were under constant monitoring by Western agencies. Once an obscure land of snake charmers, as the West saw it, India had now become the focus of Western military intelligence satellites.

One of the core areas for development by India has always been a strategic missile system. By the start of the 1980s, DRDL had developed competence in the fields of propulsion, navigation and manufacture of materials needed for missiles. It was then decided that all these technologies should be consolidated leading to the birth of the Integrated Guided Missile Development Programme (IGBM). Under this very ambitious programme we decided to create many different projects simultaneously, many of which would become household names. They were:

- Short-range surface-to-surface missile (Prithvi)
- Short-range low-level surface-to-air missile (Trishul)
- Medium-range surface-to-air missile (Akash)

- Third-generation anti-tank missile (Nag) and
- Long-range missile system (Agni).

Prithvi was the first of these missiles to be developed. Work on the missile was started in 1983, and the missile was tested successfully in 1988. By this time, the Indian defence industry had already catapulted into the top bracket of missile-manufacturing nations.

But India, who most historians agree was the pioneer of rockets and missiles during the times of Tipu Sultan, had much larger dreams. Our goal was to develop much longer range missiles, such as the IRBM (Intermediate Range Ballistic Missile) and the ICBM (Inter-Continental Ballistic Missile). Technically, IRBMs should have a range of 3000 to 5500 km; while ICBMs have a range of over 5500 km.

In this regard, perhaps the most exciting project being pursued was Agni, named after fire in Sanskrit. Agni was a long-range missile system—one comparable to any international missile system. This was the pinnacle of ambition of a nation which was dubbed as a third world nation by the Western media.

By 1987, our team had made significant breakthroughs in Agni's design and we were in a position to test a small-scale model in a simulator. One of the most critical elements which affects a missile system—especially in a long-range missile is the effect of wind. Long-range missiles such as Agni travel at hypersonic speed, which is above 5.5 Mach or over 6800 km/hour. The effect of wind shear and heat due to friction is immense and needs to be carefully measured and designed for. We had arrived at a point when we needed to test these effects of hypersonic travel on our model, study the results and design the final missile.

When Agni re-enters the atmosphere, it experiences a high enthalpy (heating) with temperature of 4000 degrees centigrade all around the heat shield and the nose cone. We had then designed a test structure using a material based on carbon-carbon which could withstand this high temperature. The problem we encountered was to simulate the external aerodynamic flow in the subsonic, supersonic and hypersonic speed regime.

To overcome this, what we now needed was a wind tunnel. A wind tunnel is a large apparatus in which you can place the model of a missile or even an aircraft component. The wind tunnel has a mechanism to generate high velocity wind within its tubes and this wind is passed over the object under test for a desired time. In this way, the scientists can observe the effect of high velocity wind on the specimen under test. Wind-tunnel tests are applied in nearly all high-speed machines—from rockets to race cars.

This is where we encountered our first roadblock. In the 1980s, while India did have wind tunnels to test sub-sonic (less than 1700 km/hour) and even supersonic (up to 2500 km/hour) flights—we were yet to develop the ability to simulate hypersonic test conditions in any wind tunnel. Developing such a wind tunnel was still at least half a decade away in the future. Agni, standing on the verge of a success, could not wait this long. Clearly, we needed to find a place outside India where we could test it, but there were few we could approach.

President Ronald Reagan (1981–89) and his administration had little trust in India. We knew any efforts for finding a test facility in the US would be futile. So, we looked elsewhere in Europe. One such link which we explored was in West Germany.

Germany had been divided into East and West after the Second World War. The two parts of the country were aligned with different political blocs—the West with the US and NATO countries, the East with the Soviet bloc. This would have a bearing on events as they unfolded. The lab we chose for our test was located in Stuttgart, a city known for its industry.

Meanwhile, our foreign affairs experts and diplomatic intelligence warned us of something ominous. In 1987 another world event was brewing. Early that year the US, Canada, France, West Germany, Japan, Italy and Britain, had started giving shape to an idea to create a 'club of elites' to stop others from developing any missile system capable of carrying a large payload—such as nuclear. They intended to achieve this by establishing strict export control of materials and knowledge. Since our plan was to make Agni capable of carrying nuclear weapons, we were reasonably sure such a restriction would affect us. We were now in a race against time before strictures were imposed by this club of elites. Stuttgart became the focus of all our efforts.

Around April that year, our talks began with the German lab. We had managed to put together a 1:100 scale model of Agni. This meant that every 1 metre of the actual missile was represented in exact proportion, in 1 cm of the model.

The model weighed a mere 20 kg and was easily transportable. We dispatched a seven-member team to Stuttgart to test the model in the hypersonic wind tunnel. Meanwhile, while the team was flying to Germany, our Delhi team finished all the necessary paperwork and documentation to ensure that the operation went smoothly. We estimated that the test and result-gathering would be completed within four days of the team landing in Stuttgart. Time was critical to us and we were doing well till that point.

We were within hours of conducting our hypersonic test when we received a jolt. The seven nations mentioned, including West Germany, signed and ratified the Missile Technology Control Regime (MTCR) curtailing all forms of knowledge and technology transfer to upcoming missile nations like us. More specifically, the 'ban' extended to all delivery systems which could deliver anything above 500 kg of payload over a distance of 300 km or more. Agni was well above these limits.

Our West German laboratory immediately came under the MTCR and refused to let us conduct the test. We tried to negotiate for the next few days, but with increasing international watch on our project it was a lost battle. Dejected, our seven-member team was recalled—the Agni model with all our efforts of half a decade was still untested. We could not go ahead with our launch.

We realized that with the MTCR in place, we were at the

mercy of the Western powers—unless we created our own capability, end-to-end, to develop our defence equipment. Under the MTCR, something as a small as a screw could be denied to us in the name of regulation and control. Clearly, our long-term interest was in creating human and technology infrastructure within our boundaries.

We were confident of our progress so far on Agni. We knew the importance of having a long-range missile for the nation's strategic strength. We also knew India, and India alone, had to find a way out of this situation. Difficulty became a breeding ground for innovation.

We now started approaching technological institutions within India. After in-depth research and discussions, we realized that this situation could be resolved only through a CFD (Computational Fluid Dynamics) solution. This was then a new field. In a nutshell, it was computerized simulation of how a fluid would behave under high speed—relevant to us as air also behaves like a fluid, especially in its flow and friction parameters.

In India of 1987–88, CFD groups were in formation stage at various institutions. We came to know that Prof. S.R. Deshpande was pioneering research in this area at the IISc (Indian Institute of Science), Bangalore. We got in touch with him and told him the challenges we were facing. Despite the obvious difficulties, he agreed. We deputed ten members of DRDL, Hyderabad, who along with Prof. Deshpande formed a CFD team for our Agni project. Then we met another hurdle.

When the CFD problem was formulated initially, the computational requirement needed very high processing powered computers. We neither had these mainframe computers in India nor the time to acquire them. We also knew that under MTCR no Western power would help us out here too.

Prof. Deshpande and the DRDL team then evolved what is called 'kinetic energy split methodology'. The problem which needed a very high computer time was elegantly solved using 1/10th of the computer time by suitably segmenting the algorithm.

Moreover, nobody had till then tried to simulate hypersonic flight in India. We ourselves were not 100% sure of the results. Air behaves remarkably differently in higher orders of speed, and its behaviour is difficult to predict even on a computer. We needed to establish some credibility for the CFD results before we could rely on data from it to deploy our Agni missile system.

So we came up with another innovation to test the results from CFD. We had already generated real flight data from the Prithvi missile system from our earlier launches. This proved to be a precious knowledge resource for Agni. Of course, the data was for lesser speeds than Agni but nevertheless useful enough. We simulated the Prithvi flight path on the computer using the same algorithm, and obtained CFD results for it. We then compared these simulation results against the actual data for Prithvi. To our delight, the results matched—giving us confidence for the Agni CFD results.

On 22 May 1989, Agni saw its first test. It had its first test flight, a successful launch in which it carried a 1000 kg payload and delivered it 800 km away. We were perhaps the first nation to develop a long-range missile system without testing in wind tunnels, and without the help of supercomputers. It was our technological leapfrog.

The experience triggered the design and development of supercomputers in the country which would finally lead to the development of PARAM, India's first supercomputer, a decade later.

*

There is more to the Agni story.

It was the night of 21-22 May 1989. There were only hours to go for the launch. Despite the technological challenges and denial of facilities we had managed to develop our own, 100% indigenous Agni missile—a world-class weapon system which could match any in the developed world. Only the acid test of missile testing remained.

The weeks preceding the test were filled with nervous excitement. We had decided to conduct the tests in the Chandipur-based Integrated Test Range (ITR). The test site was buzzing with ideas, thoughts and sometimes concerns—all leading to long and often passionate discussions. At heart, though, everybody was committed to do his best to make the project a success. Our efforts and innovation had borne great fruit, and we had almost re-invented the design process of a missile, using Computer Fluid Dynamics and simulations.

As the leader of the project I had other worries too. The US and other major powers had got an inkling of our work. While they did not have the complete picture of what we were planning, they strongly suspected that we were developing the same missile system which they had successfully managed to isolate us from a couple of years earlier. George H.W. Bush had just assumed office, and like his predecessor Ronald Reagan, he was willing to use all diplomatic means to stop India from acquiring the coveted long-range missile technology. Just a few weeks before the intended tests, we started getting reports of US spy satellites locking on to Chandipur, trying to gather all the information they could about our activities.

The date of the test was fixed for 22 May. It was known to only a handful of people. We all knew that with satellite snooping and other surveillance methods, there was a potential risk of our plans being found out well in advance. Then there were reports of the US expressing their unease with whatever was happening in Chandipur. We had won the battle against technology denial, but we were now in a race against time as we faced a diplomatic manoeuvre by a superpower.

It was 3 a.m. on the test date. We were still in the missile assembly area, fitting the last pieces on the missile, when the 'hotline' phone came on. There were no mobile phones in those days, and even long-distance calling over wired telephones was a time-consuming process. So for all critical communications, we had installed a hotline, which only top-level officers could use. A hotline call at 3 a.m., only a few hours prior to the launch, could not mean anything good.

I picked up the phone and said, 'Hello.' On the other end was Dr V.S. Arunachalam. He was the scientific advisor to the defence minister and the chief of Defence Research and Development Organization, and hence my immediate boss. Without any formalities, and in a sombre voice, he said, 'Mr Seshan wants to talk to you. Be ready. I will call back in five minutes.' The short conversation ended, but it left me with hundreds of questions. Seshan, a renowned bureaucrat, was the cabinet secretary to Prime Minister Rajiv Gandhi. A brilliant man, full of ideas, he was the seniormost bureaucrat in the nation and was known to handle complex affairs. I wondered why he would want to talk to me at 3 a.m. in the morning?

As advised by my boss, I waited near the hotline phone, occasionally shifting my glance to the large wall clock and then to the missile parts being enthusiastically ferried around by my team. Five minutes passed, then ten and then fifteen. The wait was excruciating.

Then the phone rang. I immediately caught hold of the receiver and said, 'Sir!' Both Dr Arunachalam and Seshan were on the other end. Seshan greeted me, 'Good morning, Kalam!' I reciprocated. Niceties done he immediately came to the point.

He firmly and slowly asked, 'Where are we on Agni?' Then without waiting for me to answer he said, 'We are under tremendous pressure by the US and NATO to delay any impending missile test. There are strong diplomatic channels at work.' Then almost immediately he followed again with the first question, 'Kalam! Where are we on Agni?'

It was a difficult question to answer. Of course, we were proceeding well on Agni. But his question was something else. In his question, he was also asking my suggestion on whether we should delay the test?

My mind raced vast distances in the next few seconds. There

were intelligence reports of US satellites fixing their gaze on us. I knew the US was putting increasing pressure on the Prime Minister and his office to delay the launch. Worse, there were reports that Chandipur might be struck with very bad weather in the next few days.

Then there was my team. Hard working, determined young men and women whom we had handpicked for this assignment about one decade ago. They had seen everything. Technology denials, evictions from other nations, tight budgets, media pressure and the frustration of restarting curtailed projects that had been shut down due to lack of critical apparatus. Their triumph stood in front of them—a magnificent Agni, with a tricolour painted on it. A new chapter in scientific progress and strategic power beckoned India. Should I stand down and overwrite this chapter with delay?

Strictly speaking, the missile was still in the bay. The launch could be stopped for a while. We had storage room for Agni. Maybe we would win the diplomatic war? Or some day in the near future quickly find a more conducive scenario to test Agni? This was perhaps the day for patience and accepting a small defeat of sorts, and wisdom suggested waiting for a better moment.

Or, maybe it was not a time to wait and watch but to act and achieve. I calculated all my variables and then clearing my throat said, 'Sir, the missile is at a point of no return. We cannot turn back on the test now. It is too late.' I expected a debate and a barrage of questions from my boss and Seshan. But to my surprise, as the hour hand neared 4 a.m., and the sun prepared to rise, Seshan replied, 'Okay,' and then with a deep breath and a pause. 'Go ahead.'

This was all we needed. With a heartfelt 'thank you,' I immediately kept the phone back hoping it did not ring again till we completed the test. My wish was granted.

Three hours later, we ignited the Agni missile system. The missile system, which was never tested in wind tunnels; which from its simplest screw to the complex flight control system was made within our country; the weapon system which would become the pride of a nation, was tested on 22 May 1989. It was a flawless test of hope and aspirations of a bunch of young scientists who could not be deterred by any force on this planet. We had made history.

The next day, there was a storm in Chandipur which partially destroyed our testing facility. But we all knew that we had already won the race for Agni.

PRODUCTION ATTITUDE OF A NATION

Every nation has a character, a unique attitude which governs how it deploys and develops its resources for its economic wealth. This unique attitude determines how a nation treats its natural wealth, how it skills its human resources, how it behaves when pushed into a corner by technological or economic denial by others. We will call this the Production Attitude of a Nation and it is often the critical differentiator which determines the wealth and productivity of its people.

Nations with Positive Production Attitude are open to new ideas, they handle failure better and they promote a culture of enterprise. They are characterized by supportive governance and clear ownership of intellectual and physical property. They are upwardly mobile on the learning curve; they experiment and create knowledge. They are open to partnerships on equal terms but closed to subjugation of any kind.

Nations with Negative Production Attitude have a confused identity. They end up engaged in low-cost manufacturing, or even worse end up as sub-part replication centres, and are continuously trapped in the quadrant of 'low wage—low quality—low skill and low value addition'. They are sensitive to the technological scenario outside their borders, as they are not in a position to keep pace. They may be well placed today, but their future remains uncertain, often at the mercy of the knowledge-holding nations who control their production and employment. They are essentially victims of the twenty-first century neo-imperialism and ruled by the stick of knowledge resources.

Every nation has seen an oscillation between these two Production Attitudes. For the newer nations, born in the 1900s, the journey begins as a technology follower, and then progresses towards a Positive Production Attitude. China, Japan and South Korea started off as technological consumers for the West but they quickly trained their own people and emerged as centres of Positive Production Attitude in a matter of decades. Of course, these transitions were difficult and required exemplary leadership and sometimes the pain of citizens—but nevertheless they successfully completed this transformation.

Emerging nations, such as India, who are still in the middle of this transition, often witness Positive and Negative Production Attitudes in co-existence.

For instance, we have been amongst the fastest learners, and hence shown a Positive Production Attitude, in Information Technology and Telecommunication. The IT industry's share of Indian exports increased from less than 4% in FY1998 to about 25% in 2013. India's mobile phone subscriptions have risen from less than 10 million in 2002 to 950 million in 2014.[1]

At the same time, India has seen Negative Production Attitude in many other sectors, mostly conventional, such as leather, fertilizer and tourism. India accounted for 8.8% of the world's leather trade in 1981, when China's share was less than 0.4%. In 2006, after a quarter century, India's share has fallen to 2.6% while China now accounts for over 31%.[2]

Similarly, while India imported about 10% of its fertilizer consumption till 2000-01, this increased to almost 50% in 2011-12. The total tonnage of fertilizer export increased by almost seven times.[3]

(000 tonnes of nutrients)

	2000-01	2007-08	2008-09	2009-10	2010-11	2011-12
All fertilizers (NPK)						
Imports	2,090	7,721	10,151	9148	12,363	13,002
Consumption	19,702	22,570	24,909	26,486	28,122	27,567
Share of Import in total Consumption	10.6%	34.2%	40.8%	34.5%	44.0%	47.2%

Source: Ministry of Chemicals & Fertilizers, Department of Fertilizers.

TABLE 1: Import and consumption of fertilizers in India in tonnage

Country	Number of FTAs (2013)
India	6.96 million
China (Mainland only)	55.69 million
Hong Kong (China)	25.7 million
Macau (China)	14.27 million
China (including all)	~ 95 million

TABLE 2: India vs China—Number of foreign tourist arrivals

Similar is the story of tourism, where with less than 7 million foreign tourist arrivals (FTAs) and a lowly 65th rank in travel and tourism competitiveness index of the World Economic Forum India is outnumbered by most of its Asian counterparts, as shown in table 2. India gets about 7 foreign tourists for every 100 who go to China.

The question is, how does India chart its path towards being full Positive Production Attitude in all sectors? Since the focus of this chapter is on manufacturing, we will focus more on that, but the general principles shall remain the same.

A-B-C Models

We will now discuss some unique production development models which India and other nations have followed, which determine the production attitude and hence the productivity of a nation. We will be slightly biased in naming them after Indian experiences. We call them the A-B-C models, or the Agni, BrahMos and Cola models of production.[4]

1. A-Model (The Agni Way)

We have already discussed about the Agni experience of the 1980s, and how we ended up inventing a new process of deploying Computer Fluid Dynamics (CFD) to test the hypersonic missile. This was a consequence of the constraints imposed by the Missile Technology Control Regime (MTCR), which practically shut all access to the Western laboratories to complete critical research. India then became perhaps the first nation to demonstrate the use of computerized models for obtaining accurate high-speed flight simulation data.

The Agni test of 1989 triggered a series of breakthroughs from the DRDO and its allied agencies, which ultimately culminated with India's nuclear test in May 1998. With each progress we made, the Western sanctions over what we could procure from outside our boundaries grew. Shortly after the successful test of Agni, we began the miniaturization of nuclear warheads of various yields so that they could be fitted onto missiles. This is what we called the 'Nuclear Weaponing of Agni'. It was a project which we completed piecemeal across three or four different locations for safety concerns. It was a period of very heavy sanctions on us, and we knew that we could not rely on imports for even the smallest equipment.

Fitting a nuclear warhead on a missile is a challenging task. One has to first determine the 'yield' (or the explosive power) to use. Typically, yield means the energy discharged in a nuclear reaction and is measured in TNT equivalent either in kilotons or megatons. For a perspective, 1 kiloton of TNT is equal to 4184 gigajoules.

Depending on the yield, the nuclear warhead has to be designed to occupy minimal space. Remember, that hundreds of scientists work closely with the missile and hence it is important to protect them from any potential radiation from the nuclear weapon. Hence, the nuclear warhead thus produced is designed as passive and non-hazardous in storage. There is a special mechanism which can convert it into an active and fissile state at the press of a trigger when deployed for use.

Another critical task is the mounting of the nuclear weapon inside the missile, usually at the top of the structure—on the 'nose'.

There are three critical components which need to be put in place for weaponizing a missile. First, there is a strong cylinder to hold the warhead inside the missile. Then, there is the actual warhead containing the nuclear material. And third, a series of igniter systems to activate the weapon right before it detonates.

We began with designing and developing a 400 mm long cylinder, about 500 mm in radius, which acted as a solid case to house the warhead. The main warhead was a sphere about 200 kg in weight which was carefully sealed inside this cylinder case.

The third task was installing the igniting system to activate the nuclear warhead. This step was the most difficult, especially as we were new at it. It included multiple timers, fuses and a mini-computer to control all these parts.

We were able to achieve all this without any external help. We could do so because we made the Agni missile from end-to-end by ourselves one decade ago and we also made our nuclear warhead completely indigenously.

In retrospect, if we had imported Agni from some other country, we probably would not have been able to add nuclear ability to it by ourselves. The fact that we did the original research and development, planning, analysis and production of both these critical components gave us complete know-how on how to use

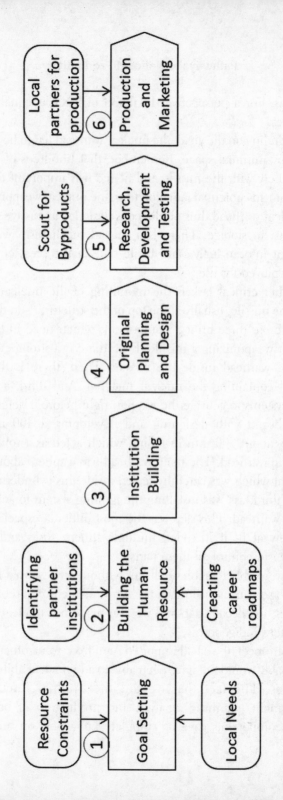

FIGURE 1: A(gni)-Model of national production

these systems. India became one of the fastest nations to install nuclear weapons on its missiles.

This is the Agni Way or the A-Model. It involves building indigenous capability such as human resources and technology to achieve the goal. The defence lab had recruited more than a hundred young scientists in the early 1980s, and it was this human resource we had built that was developing world-standard missiles one decade later and then onwards. The A-Model involves clearly identifying your specific needs, customizing them to suit your local conditions, developing the right people and institutions, using them to build the right technology and from there proceeding to planning and production.

The A-Model is indeed a difficult, sometimes even painful process of learning and re-learning, but it leads to a number of 'collateral' benefits as the nation invents a new process of production. These by-products can sometimes be as critical as the main goal themselves. The discovery of CFD, for instance, was a critical byproduct. Equally remarkable was the development of a new model of prosthetics which came out of our research for the nose cone of Agni (see box). The A-Model is imperative in conditions such as technological denial from other nations. It is also a critical path of production to follow in case a nation wants to harness a core competence which is exclusive to itself. A nation as large and diverse as India has numerous such areas of Exclusive Core Competencies (ECC) which can give it an edge in the international economy.

Agni Byproduct—Light Weight Prosthetics

Our work with Agni was enterprising and opened many new dimensions of products and processes which had significant 'collateral' benefits. One such unique product was where engineering and medical sciences converged to alleviate the pain.

During a visit to one of the hospitals in Hyderabad, we found many children were struggling to walk with artificial limbs. Upon probing further we found that the prosthetics (or artificial limbs) were weighing over 4 kg, and hence were difficult for children to carry.

At the request of Prof. B.N. Prasad of NIMS, at that time Head of the orthopaedic department, we at the Agni team wondered why we could not use the composite material used for Agni heat shield for fabricating floor reaction orthosis (FRO) for polio-affected patients. The heat shield is the material used for the nose, or the top of the missile, which faces extreme temperatures and winds when the missile reaches high speeds. Shunned by the Western powers, we developed our own carbon-carbon composite material for the nose—it was light to ensure low take-off weight and yet super strong to withstand the high temperatures and pressures.

We studied the material requirement for the prosthetics and compared it with the properties of the Agni nose material. The requirements matched the needs of the children!

The team felt the use was possible. We worked on the project for some time and came up with a FRO for the child weighing 400 gm in place of 4 kg, exactly 1/10th of the weight which the child was carrying.

The doctors helped us to fit the new lightweight FRO on the children, who started walking and running around with much more ease. Their parents were also present. There were tears of joy on many faces. With the lightweight device provided by the hospital they could run, ride a bicycle and do all sorts of things which they had been denied for a long time. It was a blissful feeling to see the children move around freely and without pain.

On the flipside, the Agni Model of Production Development is relatively slower in pace—though these impediments can be countered by rigorous multi-dimensional research institutions and close collaboration with the private sector.

2. B-Model (The BrahMos Way)

Do you know India made the world's first and so far only cruise missile which can hit targets at supersonic and even hypersonic speeds?

This is the story of BrahMos.

BrahMos Aerospace (named after two famous rivers— Brahmaputra and Moskva) was formed as a joint venture between the Defence Research and Development Organization (DRDO) and joint stock company 'Military Industrial Consortium NPO Mashino-stroyenia' (earlier known as Federal State Unitary Enterprise NPOM of Russia). The company was established in India through an inter-governmental agreement signed on 12 February 1998 between India and the Russian Federation.

BrahMos—the name evokes the fury of the Brahmaputra and the calm of the Moskva—was established with a capital of $250 million with 50.5% from the Indian side and 49.5% from the Russian side. The company is responsible for designing, developing, producing and marketing the BrahMos missile with active participation of a consortium of Indian and Russian industries.

The BrahMos marks an important point in India's defence modernization. The BrahMos missile is a two-stage vehicle that has a solid propellant booster and a liquid (propellant) ram jet system. The missile can fly at 2.8 times the speed of sound. It can carry warheads of up to 200 kg in weight and has a maximum range of 290 km. The missile is capable of being launched from multiple platforms based on land, sea, sub-sea and air.

The modular design of the missile and its capability of being launched at different orientations enables it to be integrated with a wide spectrum of platforms like warships, submarines, different types of aircraft, mobile autonomous launchers and silos.

Missile specialists state that the BrahMos is superior to the famous US Tomahawk cruise missile which is subsonic in speed. Owing to its superior performance attributes, BrahMos missiles enjoy high demand with its expected order size swelling up to

US$10 billion in the coming years (it has already reached about $7 billion). A $250 million dollar investment has yielded a business opportunity that is forty times the value!

BrahMos is a unique joint venture which has got many firsts.

The joint venture itself is a first of its kind between India and Russia to develop a world-class defence product from design to market. It is funded by two governments yet operated as a private company for faster execution of the tasks due to autonomous operation of the joint venture (JV) and empowerment.

It is the first JV to realize a weapon system with robust design and unique capabilities in various configurations which are regarded as the best in the world. It is also the first JV to have developed a universal missile for engagement of sea and land targets. For the first time in India, a missile industry consortium has been established with the participation of public and private industries who made large investments even before the placement of orders for the production of subsystems of the missile. There are as many as 205 partner industries from India and seven from Russia.

The fabrication and manufacture of subsystems of missile and ground systems has necessitated that BrahMos integrate the industries, which are drawn from several sectors of the Indian economy. Over the years, the supplier industries have grown from being small-scale entities to large manufacturers. This has not only increased employment but also generated a pool of high quality labour. Today, over 20,000 personnel are employed in industry directly or indirectly for this programme. BrahMos and the supplier industries are actively collaborating with the academia to help meet the need for skilled workers. Thus, the BrahMos has created and engaged the enhanced industry skills along with that of the diligent scientific community to strengthen national defence in particular and contribute to economic growth in general.

This is what we will call the B-Model of national production— a model based on partnerships to build core strengths.

The B-Model of National Production hinges on the ability of

the nation to identify key partners, whether other nations or foreign institutions, and on the condition that the product is a win-win for all parties. There are several 'soft powers' which come into force in such a model.

The domestic market potential of India is a major factor which can motivate external partners. As an example, in the case of Delhi Metro—the domestic demand for rolling stock (carriages in a metro train) was used to incentivize joint ventures between well-known foreign entities and Indian organizations. Within the first five years itself, these 'learning indigenous organizations' became fully capable of not only meeting Indian demand but also exporting their own rail carriages.

Similarly, unique national core competencies can be a significant bargaining power on our side. Finally, the status of relationship between the partner nations also has an important role in such a model.

The B-Model is evidently swift—as each nation is working on its core competency—something it is already a master at. The model also allows for better return on investment and economies of scale due to an expanded multi-country market. However, it has some limitations too.

First, it allows lesser flexibility for manoeuvring the product or system to the specific needs of the nation as the goal needs to be mutually beneficial. Second, it allows lesser room for experimentation and hence the scope of byproduct systems or research is limited. Third, in case there is a need for mid-course correction, the B-Model actually loses on time as there may be significant delays in getting both parties on the same page. Lastly, there is fragility to the model and it is susceptible to changes in foreign relations. Of course, some of these challenges can be handled by well-documented agreement terms based on equitable technology sharing.

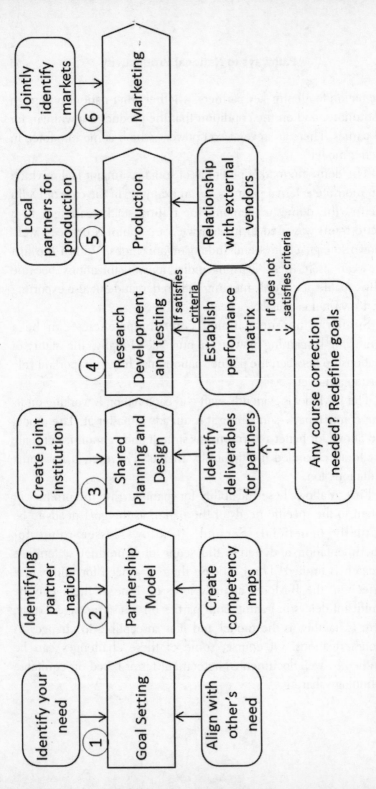

FIGURE 2: (B)rahMos-Model

3. C-Model (The Cola Way)

Coca-Cola, the world largest aerated drink company, has an interesting story. It begins with one of the fiercest wars in the history of humanity.

In 1860, just around the same time India fought its first war for independence (1857-58) from the oppression of the British, there was another battle going on against slavery right across the world—in America. In 1860, the US saw a historic presidential election in which Republican candidate Abraham Lincoln defeated three other candidates to emerge as the 16th President of the United States. Lincoln almost immediately declared his inclination to abolish slavery.

There was a clear cut division between the North and South in the US. The southern states were richer and thrived on extensive cotton cultivation. Many of them had 50% of their population as slaves—and they feared that if slavery was forbidden they would lose all their cheap agricultural labour. Thus even before Lincoln took oath as president, some of the southern states declared independence, calling themselves as the Confederate States of America.

War broke out between the Northern and slavery-opposing states called the Union and the Southern and slavery-promoting states called the Confederates. The war lasted from 1861 to 1865, till the surrender of Confederate general Robert Lee. Five days after the war was won, President Lincoln was assassinated.

The civil war remains the deadliest conflict in American history, resulting in the deaths of an estimated 750,000 soldiers and an undetermined number of civilian casualties. It is estimated that the death toll was 10% of all Northern males from 20 to 45 years old, and 30% of all Southern white males aged 18 to 40.[5]

Amongst the wounded in the war, on the Confederate side, was a man called John Pemberton. He was severely wounded in the chest by a sword strike by a Union soldier. Like many others, Pemberton was given heavy dosage of a drug, morphine, to ease his pain.

Pemberton survived the wound and the war, but he became addicted to morphine. After the war Pemberton, who was also a pharmacist, searched for a treatment for his addiction. In 1866, he started working on painkillers that would serve as drug-free alternatives to morphine. This is when he first invented the formula which would become Coca-Cola. One day, the base syrup fell by accident into carbonated water, resulting in the world's first cola. Pemberton continued to be a morphine addict, and in desperation sold his formula to his partners elsewhere in the US. Though Pemberton's formula did not work against addiction, it went on to become the world's most popular soft drink.

Coca-Cola has a unique business model, which it has maintained over a century. The company produces concentrate, which is then sold to licensed Coca-Cola bottlers throughout the world. The bottlers produce the finished product in cans and bottles from the concentrate in combination with filtered water and sweeteners. Coca-Cola's concentrate, made by Pemberton is, even today, regarded as a 'secret recipe'. According the company's website, the original recipe was only written down in 1919; until then it was passed on by 'word of mouth'. Since the 1920s, the document has sat locked in a bank. Eight decades later, Coca-Cola moved the recipe into a purpose-built vault. The company claims that only two senior executives know the formula at any given time, although they have never revealed names or positions. But according to an advertising campaign, they can't travel on the same plane.

Of course, a fraction of the story might be a marketing tactic. But the truth remains that Coca-Cola has been solely manufacturing concentrated syrup—based on a recipe invented 130 years ago. It ships this exclusive syrup to almost 200 countries across the world, where local manufacturers, unaware of the 'secret recipe', do all the low-value activities of extracting groundwater, carbonating it, mixing the syrup and bottling. Coca-Cola serves 1.8 billion servings a day, and generates revenue of over $46 billion, which is more than the GDP of more than 100 nations across the world.[6]

This is what we will call the C-Model of production of a nation.

In this model, there is an overarching reliance on original research and core technology from outside the nation, while the domestic economy just adds labour-intensive value, usually at lowest prices. The competitive strength is merely based on 'lowest hourly wages'. On the downside, such 'strength' is both short-lived and exploitative. As workers earn more, they demand better quality of life—which is the ultimate human pursuit. This means further demand for higher wages—and hence destruction of the low-cost labour advantage.

Even the story of China's manufacturing is facing these challenges. In 2014, Bank of America experts expected a wage growth in China of 11% after an estimated 10.7% gain in 2013.[7] Meanwhile, analysts at J.P.Morgan and Mizuho Securities forecast 10% to 15% increases in wages in China.[8] Driven by this loss of low cost as a competitive advantage, a number of firms, especially those making labour-intensive clothes and shoes, have begun to move to Bangladesh, Cambodia, Indonesia and Vietnam.

Nike, for example, used to make most of its sports shoes in China, but many of its big suppliers have now moved elsewhere, and towards the start of the decade, Vietnam became the company's biggest production base worldwide.[9]

In fact, Michael E. Porter, in his article, 'The Competitive Advantage of Nations', states, 'low cost of labour may bring trade into balance or surplus but lowers the nation's standard of living . . . It's the type of jobs, not just the ability to employ citizens at low wages, that is decisive for economic prosperity.'[10]

Thus the C-Model is convenient but it is risky, has short-lived gains and has an overall negative effect on the quality of life of the people of the nation. We see no advantage or sustainability in pursuing the C-Model, at least as a long-term strategy.

What about India? The reality is that in many cases, India has pursued this model for its productivity. India has amongst the lowest wage rates in the world, about two-thirds of that in China, and almost one-seventh of that in Brazil. If low-wage labour was the key, we should have been at the top of global industry—a position still only aspirational. It is not low wages but high productivity of the labour which is the key. Suppressed wages leave little morale, they curtail the ability of the working class to empower themselves with good healthcare and good education and training and therefore weigh heavily on their ability to make themselves productive.

Country	Hourly wage in manufacturing (US $)
Norway	57.5
Switzerland	51.1
Germany	44.3
Australia	39.6
France	39.0
USA	34.8
Japan	31.8
UK	29.0
Singapore	19.4
South Korea	17.9
Brazil	10.0
China	1.98
Philippines	1.85
India	1.46

TABLE 3: Average hourly wage rate in manufacturing sector

We have confused our strength of demographic dividend (due to the higher share of youth population) with our perceived asset of low-wage labour. Instead of misplaced pride in an unsustainable model of under-payment to the youth to fractionally bring down the cost of production (or service), we actually need to globally skill our youth, make them innovate and thereby acquire the ability to earn international standard wages. As we close this chapter, we recommend A and B Model of production for the nation. In cases where the follower C-Model exists—we need a national policy on finding a roadmap to upgrade it to the level of A and B in a timebound manner.

We must remember, National Productivity is never inherited— it has to be created, often painstakingly, by its citizens. Over a long run, a nation cannot sustain prosperity merely on the strength of its natural resources or its labour force or its fiscal policies and currency.

The critical ability which determines the productivity of a nation over a long period is the ability of its industries to innovate and constantly remain upwardly mobile. A strong research support, a good domestic market and enterprising competition helps national productivity stay ahead.[11]

4

BUILDING THE HUMAN RESOURCE

FROM DEMOGRAPHIC DIVIDEND TO
ACTUAL ADVANTAGE

If India truly wants to be the creator of world-class services and products one key aspect will be to transform the human resource of the nation.

It is indisputable that India possesses the most promising demographic trends. Currently, the supply of skilled manpower in India is approximately 3.1 million per year.[1] According to the ILO, there will be a demand for 500 million skilled workers in India by 2022. This wide gap of 500 million skilled workers needs to be filled in eight years; more than 60 million skilled workers every year. But even in 2022, the average age of India would be 29 years, with more than 650 million people in the working age group. Thus India, by 2022, can not only meet its own demand but also cater to the global labour demand, which will be significant—especially with an ageing China—whose average age in 2022 will be over 37 years.[2] It is estimated that by 2016 onwards, every fourth skilled worker added in the global workforce can be an Indian. By 2025, India will be home to almost one-third of the world's youth.

But that is only the quantity aspect. Where we are needing critical action is the issue of the quality of the Indian education system. There are three simple aspects which are important to the success of any human resource, whether it be in an organization, state or a whole nation.

1) Quality of school education
2) Developing knowledge resources
3) Employability of the youth
4) Quality of research
5) State of health

It is easy to see the correlation in them. A well-balanced education system leads to creative youth, who can either go into research or become part of the skill force. Good research is the pillar to creating an eco-system where the nation can design, develop and produce all by itself. All this is possible only when the workforce is healthy. Let us analyse these aspects in more depth.

1. QUALITY OF SCHOOL EDUCATION

In 2009, India cautiously agreed to participate in the PISA evaluation programme—putting it through only two of its states, Himachal Pradesh and Tamil Nadu, both top-performing states in education.

PISA, or the Programme for International Student Assessment, evaluates education systems in seventy countries by testing the academic abilities of 15-year-old students in each country. Skills and knowledge that the students have acquired at the end of compulsory education in reading, math, problem solving and scientific literacy are tested. It has become a definitive standard for the judging nations in how well their children are performing in practical learning, rather than just relying on literacy rate figures.

The results were disturbing.

- In reading, of the 74 regions participating in PISA 2009 or 2009+ these two states beat out only Kyrgyzstan.
- In mathematics, of the 74 regions participating; the two states finished second and third from the last, again beating only Kyrgyzstan.

- In science, the results were even worse, Himachal Pradesh came in very last, behind Kyrgyzstan, while Tamil Nadu inched ahead to finish 72nd of 74.

We do not subscribe to the ideology that private schooling will be able to supplement and make up for the shortcomings in government schools. It is a design-to-fail strategy—as the numbers would never add up. Education is a basic right, now even legally, and it is the responsibility of the government, both state and central, to ensure that it comes up to standards.

Solving the education challenge is a multipronged issue which begins at the level of the teachers, who are the most important resource in an educational system.

First, is the broader issue of 'choice' in school. This can be achieved by a system of school vouchers. What it means is that economically and social backward communities are not assigned a school in their neighbourhood, but rather given a school voucher which they can use in any government or even private school of their choice. The idea is that parents will choose the optimal school for their children—and enrolment in a school will also reflect their assessment of it. Thus at a policy and administration level one can rate the performance of a particular government or government-aided school by simply seeing the enrolment pattern in it. This could be linked to incentives, grants and teacher assessment. Such a programme exists in many parts of the world, including the US. One such pilot case was done by the Andhra Pradesh School Choice Project that was based on randomized trials. This was conducted by the Massachusetts Institute of Technology's Abdul Latif Jameel Poverty Action Lab (J-PAL) and the results were very promising. It would be prudent to see how such a school voucher programme can be linked with the Right to Education Act.[3]

In 2015, Srijan and I went to the Malti Gyanpeeth Puraskar 2015 where I had been invited to present awards to fifteen teachers from the government schools of Punjab. The award is named after

Malti Mohinder Singh Syngle, who is 93 years old and has been a career educationist and a teacher. Thousands of teachers apply for the award. These are judged by an esteemed jury to decide on the final fifteen awardees. It is a unique way in which a highly experienced school teacher, in her nineties, has collaborated with the state government to motivate teachers. We are confident that such a model of recognizing great government school teachers, and hence motivating them, can be replicated elsewhere too.

Another important element of the school education system are the principals, who not only teach but also manage other teachers and school resources. How can we empower these principals across the government, especially rural schools? In 2014, both of us visited Bagar district of Rajasthan to meet the Piramal Fellows and see their work. The Piramal Fellowship, formerly called the Gandhi Fellowship, is a unique two-year programme where young university graduates and professionals are assigned the task of working in a rural area for two years. A bulk of their work involves working with the school principals, on the premise that those who help shape students can also shape society. We met about fifty such young boys and girls, who were from across India and even abroad, and were living in the villages. We also met a set of school principals with whom these young fellows were working and it was enthralling to see how these principals praised the efforts of the Piramal Fellows. Some of them also showed us some educational games which the fellows had developed with the headmasters and principals. One of them, which was particularly impressive, was a snake and ladder game improvised to improve teaching of math to children. It was instructive to see how these young professionals, in their tenure of two years to village services, were helping transform the principals and headmasters and thereby changing education in a way few could conceive.

Can we evolve a permanent and more nationally scaled model from this initiative? We both thought about it and came up with an idea of starting an Indian Teaching Services, or ITS. This can be on similar lines to the IAS, IPS or other highly reputed government services managed by the UPSC.

It should be open to educated and highly qualified youth who wish to take school education and curricular transformation as a lifetime subject. ITS officers should be treated at par with IAS officers and assigned the work of transforming education policy at national and state level and education delivery at district level. The service should see the same level of competition and excellence as other services managed by the UPSC, with people from multi-disciplinary areas applying for it. It should be seen as a sought-after career option, with emphasis on continuous learning and knowledge updating. Its officers should be in charge of all education budgets, school infrastructure and vocational education. They would be responsible for upgradation of school syllabus, regular training of teachers, school hardware procurement and examination patterns. Later, with time they can also be assigned other higher education and research areas. Poor literacy and low level of education are the greatest battle we need to fight in the 21st century and to win we need dedicated and specialist warriors which the ITS can provide.

2. DEVELOPING KNOWLEDGE RESOURCES

In 1970s, Buckminster Fuller, the famous polymath, created the 'Knowledge Doubling Curve' to analyse how much time it takes for knowledge to double in the world. He noticed that up until 1900 the total human knowledge doubled approximately every century. By the end of World War II, in 1945, knowledge was doubling every 25 years.[4]

Things are much different now. Former Google CEO Eric Schmidt says, 'Between the birth of the world and early 2000s, five exabytes or 5000 terabytes of information was created. We now create five exabytes every two days.' In the new century, knowledge creation is not a simple affair as different types of knowledge have different rates of growth. For instance new biological data, such as knowledge about stem cells, genetics and bio-engineering, doubles every nine months.[5] Nanotechnology knowledge is doubling every two years and clinical knowledge every 18 months. Overall, on average human knowledge is doubling every 13 months. More video is uploaded to YouTube in 60 days than the three major TV networks have created in the last 60 years. Its users upload more than 24 hours of video to YouTube every minute of every day. Our knowledge of medicine doubles every two years.

What about the future? According to IBM, in the next decade, in a world where most humans and gadgets will be connected to the internet, the doubling of knowledge will occur every 12 hours.[6]

Today the internet is estimated to be 5 million terabytes (TB) of which Google has indexed roughly 200 TB or just .004% of its total size. Nations which invest in knowledge management and technologies stand to be the leaders in global manufacturing and services.

While new knowledge is created it is also rendering old knowledge useless—knowledge decay is occurring at the rate of 30% in hi-tech areas.[7] If knowledge doubles every year while this decay happens, it means that if you are an expert on a topic today, and you do not update yourself continuously, within the next four years your knowledge would be completely outdated and meaningless. What applies for a person, also applies for a whole society and nation. Nimble and agile societies, which not only encourage accumulation but also updation of knowledge, are going to be the winners of the future. Those who fail to keep up will be subservient labourers to the bearers of knowledge resources.

3. EMPLOYABILITY OF THE YOUTH

The difficult state of availability of skilled manpower can be largely attributed to the Indian education system, which does not focus on training students in employable skills. The Indian education system's focus has been more on theory and less on practical training, which helps in developing employable 'skills'. Equally important is upgrading skills. Today, a large section of India's labour force carries out tasks with outdated skills.

It is imperative to take necessary steps to ensure employability of the human resource. For instance, although equipped with 14 lakh engineering seats across the nation, 82% of the total engineering graduates are deemed to be unemployable. Even large IT companies such as TCS, Wipro and Infosys have dedicated campuses of their own where fresh engineering graduates are re-trained in skills which are employable. Up to six months of training is needed before the already qualified engineers can be made job ready, which leaves one with questions about the curriculum in the four-year engineering course itself. One of the authors of this book happened to interview the director of one such campus in south India, who said, 'We treat the incomers (fresh engineers) as completely raw. We ask them to take an initial test covering their engineering curriculum, and separate them into two streams. The top stream has reasonable knowledge expected from a fresh engineer. The other stream is sometimes almost as nascent as 12th graders in applicable knowledge—we need to completely review their basic understanding of engineering itself. I wonder what are the colleges teaching them. The only salvation is that these chaps pick up skills quick.' Before ending he added, 'The bottom stream is almost 80% of our fresh recruits.'

Unless this quality issue is addressed, any form of industrialization initiative in India, such as Make in India, will yield only low-level employment for the Indian youth, while the complex operations will have to be handled by an expat workforce.

Unless the workforce upgrades its skill-sets, it is at the risk of being rendered irrelevant in the new-age economy.

Global Human Resource Cadre

How to generate time-bound employable skill force, is the question that arises. The Indian skill development programme has to focus on employability. It is reported that in a decade's time, India will need 500 million employable skilled youth. Hence, there is a need to completely change the university education syllabus and the secondary school education syllabus.

In the secondary school syllabus for the 9th, 10th, 11th, 12th classes, 25% of the time has to be allotted for a skill development programme. When the secondary school students come out from the school, they will have two certificates; one for 10+2 qualification, and the other for the unique skill acquired during the four-year period. That means we get every year a skilled workforce bank of almost 7 million.

In a knowledge society, the workers instead of being skilled or semi-skilled will be knowledgeable and have flexibility in the work they can do.

A skilled worker has to be a life-long learner with continuously upgraded skills for management of shop floor, workshop, or multi-disciplinary skill-force. The skilled worker can also dream of becoming an engineering graduate, management graduate, or even the chief executive of the firm.

A three-pronged strategy is needed to make education more attractive, make it skill imparting and simultaneously create employment potential. How do we do that?

First, the educational system should highlight the importance of entrepreneurship and orient the students towards setting up enterprises which will provide them an outlet for creativity, freedom and ability to generate wealth. Diversity of skills, ability to handle difficult situations and sheer perseverance in work makes an entrepreneur. These are attributes that should be taught to all the students. In addition, college syllabi even for arts, science, and commerce courses should include topics and practicals where such entrepreneurship is possible.

Secondly, the banking system should provide venture capital right from the village level to the prospective entrepreneurs for undertaking new enterprises. When we studied the performance of a venture fund of a leading private bank, we found a few entrepreneurs had increased their profitability manifold in less than seven years generating thousands of direct jobs and tens of thousands of indirect jobs. We need a large number of such venture capital institutions that can share the risk and promote entrepreneurs, especially with investment in the micro financing band. The educational system can bring out the success stories in the form of documents highlighting venture capital funding and employment generation opportunities across the world.

Thirdly, entrepreneurs have to produce competitive products for becoming successful in their missions. The experts here may like to study the role of education in improving the competitiveness index rating of the country to within ten ranks.

4. QUALITY OF RESEARCH

Research and Education need to be integrated to create new dimensions of skill sets and this would require significantly higher spending on research from the current $36 billion, which is less than 1% of GDP.

In 2012, China spent $296 billion on research and development, just under 2% of its gross domestic product. The same year, the US spent $405 billion, or 2.7% of its GDP. Asia's well known growth stories of Japan and South Korea spend even higher, 3.7% and 4.4% of their GDP on R&D respectively.

A democracy such as India is most conducive to breeding new innovations, but with the lack of proper IPR regime and enforcement, the space remains untapped. But is spending the only gap which separates India from the being a vibrant research society?

Table 1 shows in detail the state of patent filings in the world, a good measure of the intellectual property being created. Patents are rights given under law to an inventor for a limited period for detailed disclosure of the invention. In this time, the inventor can commercially use the product almost exclusively. Once the grant period expires, usually around seven years, the process can be used by anyone for commercial purposes. Most of the inventions around us were patented by their inventors.

Table 1 shows two aspects. First it ranks nations based on the total number of patents applied, or patents filed, by people of its nationality. But not every patent filed is accepted. Once a patent application is accepted a patent is granted. The second aspect which the table does is to rank nations based on the total number of patents granted to it. It shows that of the total patents filed globally just about 1% were filed by Indians, placing India at 14th position. Comparatively, China's share has risen to 28%, standing at the top position. What is more alarming is that when we compare the patents granted column, India's share in this column is 0.4%, placing it at 21st position, just above Iran. China's share here is 13%, placing it at the third position. In terms of patents granted, Japan tops the list, with 28% of worldwide patents granted going to Japanese people. It is a matter of concern that a nation with one-sixth the global population is able to create only one in every 250 patents worldwide.

But there is more. Table 2 adds another column to the patent grant list—the overall expenditure the nation incurs every year on research. The last column in this table divides this total research spend by the total patents granted to compare the expenditure per patent granted for each of the fourteen nations in table 1. A few interesting trends emerge:

a) Six out of the thirteen nations above India in the list spend less on their Research and Development compared to India.
b) Switzerland spends one-fifth of what India does on Research and Development but generates five times the number of patents.
c) In the list of fourteen nations, India spends the maximum, close to 8.22 million, for every patent granted. This is eighteen times more than what Japan has to spend for each patent as a part of its Research and Development expenditure.

So, the Research and Development budget is not the only issue which affects our research ability. The issue is also one of effectively utilizing resources which are already committed to the sector.

Rank in patents filed	Applicant's origin country	Patents filed (2013)	Share in total patents filed	Rank in patents granted	Patents granted (2013)	Share in total patents granted
1	China	734,096	28%	3	154,489	13%
2	USA	501,162	19%	2	243,986	20%
3	Japan	473,141	18%	1	340,303	28%
4	South Korea	223,527	9%	4	123,820	10%
5	Germany	184,493	7%	5	81,635	7%
6	France	71,083	3%	6	43,060	4%
7	UK	51,300	2%	8	20,941	2%
8	Switzerland	44,997	2%	9	20,168	2%
9	Russia	34,067	1%	7	23,365	2%
10	Netherlands	33,589	1%	11	16,671	1%

Rank in patents filed	Applicant's origin country	Patents filed (2013)	Share in total patents filed	Rank in patents granted	Patents granted (2013)	Share in total patents granted
11	Italy	28,896	1%	10	19,313	2%
12	Canada	26,304	1%	12	13,407	1%
13	Sweden	22,647	1%	13	12,267	1%
14	India	20,908	1%	21	4,390	0.4%

TABLE 1: Rank of various countries in terms of patents filed and granted[8]

Applicant's origin country	Rank in patents granted	Patents granted (2013)	Share in total patents granted	Expenditure on R&D (US$ billion PPP)	Expenditure on R&D (as a % of GDP)	Expenditure in US$ million (PPP) for every patent granted
Japan	1	340,303	28%	160.3	3.67%	0.47
USA	2	243,986	20%	405.3	2.70%	1.66
China	3	154,489	13%	337.5	2.08%	2.18
South Korea	4	123,820	10%	65.4	4.36%	0.53
Germany	5	81,635	7%	69.5	2.30%	0.85
France	6	43,060	4%	42.2	1.90%	0.98
Russia	7	23,365	2%	32.8	1.00%	1.40
UK	8	20,941	2%	38.4	1.70%	1.83
Switzerland	9	20,168	2%	7.5	2.30%	0.37
Italy	10	19,313	2%	19	1.10%	0.98
Netherlands	11	16,671	1%	10.8	1.60%	0.65
Canada	12	13,407	1%	24.3	1.80%	1.81
Sweden	13	12,267	1%	11.9	3.30%	0.97
India	21	4,390	0.40%	36.1	0.90%	8.22

TABLE 2: Expenditure-related data for patents filed by different countries[9]

India has thirty-seven laboratories under the Council of Scientific and Industrial Research (CSIR), each dedicated to a specific branch of application science. It has numerous IITs, IIMs, the DRDO, the Indian Institute of Science and many other institutions which can emerge as leading centres of research in the world.

Together we have interviewed many scientists from laboratories across the nation. We have also seen many industries across the spectrum. One thing is clear, there is a visible disconnect between industry and laboratories. Laboratories are working aloof to the contemporary needs of the industry, often solely relying on government funding and auto-discretion on what R&D to pursue. On the other hand, industry seems to be operating in a research-free mode. Most industries treat indigenous research as an expense and not as an investment. The time has arrived, or perhaps is already overdue, for the industry and research to come together and jointly work on mission-mode research leading to products and services which have commercial viability and industrial application.

A well-guided and supported research can be the greatest asset to a nation's economy. The most significant case of such collaboration is happening since 2009.

In 2008, beginning with the housing bubble burst, the US economy plunged into an unprecedented depression, affecting almost all nations in the world. Between February 2008 and February 2010, the US lost about 8.7 million jobs. The GDP contracted by 5.1%.[10] Many started wondering whether it was the end of US economic dominance.

But while all this was happening, away from the limelight, US researchers and universities were working overtime to invent methods to economically harness a new form of energy—shale gas. This is natural gas trapped inside rocks, especially sedimentary rocks. Till 2009, the method used to extract this gas was costly and made shale gas economically unviable. But in 2009-10, a new method of hydraulic fracturing made the extraction much easier—leading to a new form of energy industry in the US.

While the economy continued to sputter, shale oil production began to soar. It rose relatively consistently through 2013 and then really took off, hitting 8.5 million barrels per day. Meanwhile, imports of energy and gas began to plummet, dropping to 7.17 million barrels per day, the lowest point in almost two decades. In fact, according to a report from the IHS Global Insight in December 2011, shale gas production accounted for 600,000 jobs in 2010, barely one year after the 'official' end of the recession. And the increase in natural gas production in turn led to lower electricity prices, fostering a revival in the chemical, steel, and manufacturing sectors and creating thousands of jobs. A focused research in extraction of shale gas has brought energy abundance and economic growth in the US—at a time when things were looking bleak.

In 2015, we visited the Texas Instruments office in Bangalore for an event where they had gathered young engineering students from across India to showcase their solutions for societal challenges. There we were told that Texas Instruments, a US-based company, runs a rigorous university connect programme, which benefits over 200,000 students every year in Asia alone. Their worldwide numbers are even more impressive—they connect with over 500,000 students per year in over 7,000 labs in 2625 universities. We were impressed to see the outreach into academia by industry in this way.

It is time for our laboratories, universities and industries to work together on joint goals. Indian companies need to reach out to academia and students in colleges to work with them on contemporary subjects. Research labs need to interface more with industries in their domain to ensure they work on what is applicable and needed and their patents are useful to manufacturers. College teachers and students need to work on case studies which are relevant to the Indian scenario. The policy makers need to review and revise syllabi every three years to suit the changing global knowledge context.

In 8th century BCE, about 2700 years ago, Indian civilization was the first to build a dedicated centre of learning, similar to the modern-day university town, in Taxila.[11] This is the place where Kautilya composed his famous work *Arthashastra*, Charaka studied Ayurveda and Panini invented Sanskrit grammar. In the 5th century, 1500 years ago, Indians established a much more elaborate university at Nalanda which would attract many foreign scholars with its modern outlook and research focus. However, Indian academia and education in general have seen a downward trend since 1200 CE, with the destruction of Nalanda, and a general decline in standards.

Hiuen Tsang, the Chinese academician, and perhaps the most famous of the foreign scholars who studied in Nalanda, said in admiration of the Indian education system: 'The teachers must themselves have closely studied the deep and secret principles they contain, and penetrated to their remotest meaning. They then explain their general sense, and guide their pupils in understanding the words which are difficult. They urge them on and skilfully conduct them. They add lustre to their poor knowledge and stimulate the desponding.'[12]

It is time India reinvents its teachers, its education and research system to create the global standard workforce and world-leading research which the people of the nation deserve—the one which can add lustre and stimulate even the desponding.

5

ENSURING A HEALTHY NATION FOR ALL

STATE OF HEALTH

Life expectancy in India rose to 65 years in 2012 from 32 years at the time of independence in 1947. Even then India's infant mortality rate—50 deaths for every 1000 births—remains among the highest in the world. Almost half of the country's children under five are classed as chronically malnourished, and more than a third of Indians aged between 15 to 49 are undernourished, according to India's National Family Health Survey.[1] A 2011 *Wall Street Journal* investigation into India's government-run healthcare system described public hospitals as 'out of date, short-staffed and filthy'.[2]

No society can be productive without being healthy. Good health, measured as a composite of life expectancy, infant and maternal mortality rates, state of malnourishment, vaccination coverage, health awareness and disease incidence is a critical parameter of a nation's well-being and its economic growth. Healthcare is even more of a challenge with the poor and those out of access to services and connectivity, who are more vulnerable to disease. Where do we stand on this front?

The truth is, India's focus on healthcare is mediocre compared to other nations.

Country/ Region	Share of Health-care expense (% of GDP)	Healthcare expense (per capita (2012) PPP US$	Times the healthcare expense per capita compared to India
India	4.05%	61	1
South Asia	3.97%	56	0.9
China	5.41%	321	5.3
Brazil	9.31%	1056	17.3
Russia	6.26%	886	14.5
USA	17.91%	8895	145.8
High-Income Countries	12.22%	4635	76.0
Sub-Sahara	6.46%	96	1.6
World	10.19%	1030	16.9

TABLE 1: Share of healthcare in the GDP for different countries and healthcare expense per capita and its comparison to India

A good measure of a nation's focus on its citizens' health is measured by the share of GDP which goes into healthcare. Table 1 shows the share of total healthcare in the GDP across various regions and nations. It also shows the per capita healthcare expenditure. The last column compares a nation's per capita healthcare expenditure to that of India. Our per capita healthcare expense is US$ 61 per year and we spend nearly 4% of the total GDP in healthcare (private and public). Only the figures for the rest of South Asia are comparable to that number. China spends 5.4% of its much larger GDP—and hence spends more than five times on its per capita health as India does. Amongst other BRIC nations, Brazil spends over 17 times and Russia nearly 15 times. Even the poorest nations in Sub-Saharan Africa spend 6.5% of their GDP on healthcare. The world on an average spends 17 times more on healthcare per person compared to India. We, with our

South Asian friends, are clearly an outlier in the global healthcare scenario.

Even for South Asia, the low number is largely due to Bangladesh's low healthcare expenditure (at $25 per capita). However, even with those numbers, Bangladesh has managed respectable health parameters thanks to an efficient and targeted public health programme.

Healthcare in India essentially comprises three segments.

The first segment consists of the government-sponsored public health system, which includes government hospitals, primary and secondary health centres, and nutrition-related centres such as mid-day meal centres like anganwadis.

The second segment consists of the high-cost private sector healthcare which has expanded as a major enterprise opportunity everywhere in the country, especially metro cities.

The third segment is a bridge between the first and second. It consists of healthcare which is private in ownership but is affordable, though often at the cost of quality.

The first segment is under explosive pressure with unimaginable patient-to-doctor ratios. A duty day for a typical government resident doctor, in a full-fledged government hospital, means 24 straight hours of emergency/casualty posting and operation theatre service and responding to emergency call. Not only the doctors, but also the paramedic staff and infrastructure are stretched beyond their designed capacity—leading to significant quality issues. Primary Health Centres (PHCs), India's government-funded centres for basic healthcare, including deliveries, are suffering a different problem altogether. Unlike hospitals, which are in the limelight and in constant use by the public, PHCs tend to be affected by the obscurity of being in villages, combined with a lack of basic infrastructure such as electricity. Surveys have found absenteeism between 35 and 58% in PHCs, depending on which state is being surveyed.[3]

In the second segment are highly sophisticated healthcare

centres—often funded by equity and operating usually at high standards. They are beyond the affordability of three-quarters of the population, but still give healthcare at lower cost as compared to the West—thereby attracting health tourism. However, they have also been under scrutiny for inducing what we call 'diagnostic pain'—recommending unnecessary diagnostics, medicines and expensive surgeries.

We met a friend of ours who runs a famous hospital in southern India. He told us about how he is having difficult in keeping his hospital afloat. He said, 'We got some investors in the hospital who picked up a large stake. This money helped us buy modern equipment. Back then our return on interest was 14%.' However, things were now different. 'Today the investor is demanding 20% return on investment. We cannot give this much profit from our hospital—unless we start extracting money from patients by recommending them unnecessary procedures and inflate their expenses. It would be highly unethical.'

Not everyone would stick to ethics over profits in such cases. A study in Chennai revealed that 47% of the total deliveries performed in a private hospital ended up in high-cost caesarean operations. The same figure for government/public hospitals stood at 20%.[4] One inference can be that private hospitals were conducting surgeries two and a half times more often than government hospitals, many of which could have been avoided.

The third or the bridge segment is a segment of true diversity. It is a conglomeration ranging from charitable hospitals, run by trusts, to doctors, often with dubious degrees. There are shining examples of innovation in low-cost quality care such as Aravind (for eyes) in this segment. At the same time, it is also true that there are about 2.5 million 'quacks' or illegal medical practitioners operating in towns and villages. Nevertheless, this segment has been the face saver of India's healthcare services.

Historically, India has had a great record of healthcare, and its innovations in the sector are well known. Throughout history, healthcare has been a fundamental responsibility of the state. The Indus Valley Civilization perhaps was a pioneer in promoting public healthcare services, when they established the Great Bath at Mohenjo-daro in third millennium BCE. Fa-hien (CE 405–411), a Chinese traveller who visited India during the times of Chandragupta, provided details about the charitable dispensaries in Pataliputra. According to his account, 'the nobles and householders of this country founded hospitals within the city to which the destitute of all countries, the poor, the crippled and the diseased may come. Here, these people were treated freely and provided with every kind of help.'[5]

Much later, in CE 1595, Sultan Muhammad Qutab Shah IV built a hospital known as Dar-u-Shifa (the house of cure) on the banks of the Mossi river. It had accommodation for 4000 patients and physicians to treat them. It was perhaps the biggest hospital in the world, all managed by the state.

India's healthcare system saw a rapid decline under the British — with decline in number and quality of the public health services. The nation soon lost its ability to cope with diseases and outbreaks were frequent eroding the scope and significance of the services. We have already seen that the healthcare spend in India is surprisingly low compared to other countries. We will explore this subject further taking up the issue of public healthcare alone.

Table 2 uses the previous table 1 and substitutes the figures only for public per capita healthcare spending (instead of total healthcare spending). The results are disquieting.

India not only spends amongst the least in overall healthcare spending per capita as shown in the previous table, it scores even poorer on public healthcare spending—merely one-third comes from public healthcare spending out of the overall healthcare spend. This time again, the only companions we have are in South Asia—perhaps arising from the same colonial lineage. This time Brazil's per capita public healthcare spending is 24 times ours, Russia's stands at 27 times. The average world citizen gets almost

Country/Region	Share of public healthcare in overall health expenditure	Share of public healthcare expense (% of GDP)	Public healthcare expense per capita (2012) PP (US$)	Times the public healthcare expense per capita compared to India
India	33%	1.3%	20	1.0
South Asia	33%	1.3%	19	0.9
China	56%	3.0%	179	8.9
Brazil	46.4%	4.3%	490	24.3
Russia	61%	3.8%	540	26.8
USA	46.4%	8.3%	4126	204.4
High Income Countries	61.4%	7.5%	2847	141.1
Sub-Sahara	44%	2.8%	42	2.1
World	59.8%	6.1%	615	30.5

TABLE 2: Public per capita healthcare spending pattern across countries and their comparison with India

31 times more expenditure from his or her government as compared to an average Indian. We need a healthcare reboot.

In fact, going by the data from the World Bank, only sixteen countries, from over 220 nations across the world, have lesser share of public healthcare expenditure than India. Even among these, only eleven have lesser per capita public healthcare expenditure than India. These are mostly war- or unrest-ravaged countries— Afghanistan, Pakistan, Haiti, Uganda, Myanmar, Sierra Leone, Guinea, Tajikistan, Cambodia, Liberia and Chad.[6] Nations considered extremely poor, such as Nigeria, Sudan, Georgia and Yemen, have higher per capita public healthcare expenditure than India.

First, on a broad note, we need to increase our focus on healthcare spending, more specifically public funding in healthcare. By no means do we advocate achieving a level near the high-income countries, but surely our public spending on healthcare needs to be above 3% of the GDP and the total healthcare spend should be propelled above 6% of the GDP. This will also ensure a healthy 50% of total healthcare coming from the public sector. The World Health Organization (WHO) says that 'the estimated economic loss for India due to deaths caused by all the diseases in 2005 was 1.3% of its GDP'.[7] It is further estimated that with an increase in the number of non-communicable diseases, such as cancer, this loss is expected to increase to 5% of GDP by 2015–16 if it is not checked.[8]

Even if we assume that half of this GDP loss can be saved, India stands to gain 2.5% additional GDP growth every year, by an increase of less than 2% of GDP in the overall healthcare budget. A worthy investment to make, even considered on purely economic terms. Of course, a healthy and long life is the most important factor for happy living to all citizens—the primary goal of any nation.

Second, there is a need to focus on preventive healthcare rather than curative. India is home to the world's second largest population and the largest number of youth, hence it has the greatest stake in the future of humankind. We need to predict, analyse and prepare for the future ailments which will affect humanity. The world, and India alike, is facing a growing threat from new diseases that are jumping the human-animal species barrier as a result of environmental disruption, global warming and the progressive urbanization of the planet, as feared. At least forty-five diseases that have passed from animals to humans have been reported in the last two decades,[9] with the number expected to escalate in the coming years. Together with Antimicrobial resistance (AMR) animal-origin microbes infecting humans which threaten humanity like never before.[10] There is no treatment, cure or vaccine, or the possibility of effective prevention or control of most animal-origin microbes. In addition, the uncontrolled and inappropriate use of antibiotics has resulted in increased antimicrobial resistance and is seriously threatening drug-control strategies against even common diseases.

In 1948, the U.S. Secretary of State pronounced that the conquest of all infectious diseases was imminent.[11] Twenty years later, the US Surgeon General declared victory: 'The war against diseases has been won.'[12] The overconfidence of the time was understandable. Scientists had conquered polio, nearly eradicated smallpox, developed childhood vaccinations, and assembled an arsenal of more than 25,000 different 'miracle drug' antibiotic preparations.[13] But that was it. The year smallpox was declared history, a virus called human immunodeficiency virus began its colonization of Africa and the world with HIV/AIDS. In some countries, the prevalence of HIV now exceeds 25% of the adult population.[14] The malaria parasites are now antibiotic-resistant, and the mosquitoes carrying them are insecticide-resistant as well. Even the diseases once thought subdued are fighting back with renewed ferocity. Infectious disease remains the number one killer of children worldwide.

Since about 1975, previously unknown diseases have surfaced at a pace unheard of in the annals of medicine—more than thirty new diseases in thirty years, most of them newly discovered viruses. What is happening? Why is it getting worse?[15] To answer that question, we first have to consider where these diseases are coming from, since they have to come from somewhere. In other words, from where do emerging diseases emerge? An increasingly broad consensus of infectious disease specialists have concluded that 'nearly all' of the increasingly frequent emergent disease episodes have come to us from increased exposure to the animal world and is compounded by the ever increasing contact between humans as a result of globalization.[16]

Tuberculosis, called 'the captain of all these men of death', had been acquired through the domestication of goats. In the 20th century, TB killed approximately 100 million people.[17] Measles came from domesticated cows, a mutant of the bovine rinderpest virus. The measles virus has so successfully adapted to humans that cattle cannot get measles and we cannot get rinderpest. Only with the prolonged intimate contact of domestication was the rinderpest virus able to mutate enough to make the jump. Measles is now considered a benign disease but not before about 200 million people worldwide in the last 150 years succumbed to it.[18] Leprosy came from the water buffalo, the cold virus from horses. If we look at the animal kingdom—from goats, sheep, camels, poultry, all fish, with whom human beings are in regular contact—they each have probably 30 or 40 major diseases, and the possibility for exposure is huge. As the custodian of the health of one-sixth of humanity, we need to reconsider our contemporary healthcare regime from the very root.

Can one such care be immunity as part of healthcare management itself? Immunology has been studied and understood in the context of the compelling problems of infectious disease. But the rapidly growing knowledge of immune interactions with the healthy bacteria living inside our bodies, and the many benefits they confer, suggests an alternative view. Mechanisms of defence against pathogens are one aspect of a complex system with the broader purpose of managing our healthy bacteria. From this perspective, adaptive immunity may be viewed as a flexible system for simultaneously recruiting and managing a near limitless number of potential microbes who would entirely depend on each other for survival. This perspective can allow for re-interpretation of many observations and can suggest new experiments to help us better understand our complex interactions with the microbes that surround us. Other simpler preventive healthcare measures could be promoting exercise, yoga, meditation and healthier eating and lifestyle, especially amongst children.

Third, we need original research and to think beyond producing existing drugs cheaper—popularly called generic drugs. We were studying a special dataset by the World Health Organization regarding the Top 10 causes of death spread across income groups of nations. We saw some interesting trends.

When we studied the lower middle income nations, to which India also belongs, the top ten causes of death were[19]

1. Heart disease
2. Stroke
3. Lower respiratory infections caused due to indoor air pollution
4. COPD
5. Diarrhoea
6. Birth complications
7. HIV
8. Diabetes
9. Tuberculosis
10. Cirrhosis of liver due to liquor consumption or otherwise.

These are the top ten killers of more than half the world, which falls in the low- to middle-income group, especially in India and China.

We then focused our attention on the high-income nations, such as the US and Europe and their top ten causes of death. These are nations where original medical research is being conducted. They are:[20]

1. Heart disease
2. Stroke
3. Trachea Brochus
4. Alzheimer's
5. COPD
6. Lower respiratory infections
7. Colon cancer
8. Diabetes
9. Hypertensive heart disease
10. Breast cancer.

Notice that 50% of the top ten causes of death in the low- to middle-income nations do not find a place in the list of causes in the high-income countries. Moreover, even for causes such as heart disease and stroke, the reasons and hence the cure to be followed in the two groups is different. Hence, our diseases and the cures needed are different.

Today most original research in medical science is located in the high-income nations. Original research on pathology in India is nascent and needs development. Why are we saying this? It is because we cannot expect and wait for research of diseases which affect our people to come from nations who are not affected by these ailments. It is time for our medical community, research facilities and government to stand up for original research to help our people. India, with its highly educated youth population, with some of the best centres of medical learning, has a unique opportunity to champion original research from disease to drug, not only for itself, but all low- and middle-income nations. Research and healthcare spending need to find convergence here.

Lastly, we are facing a different set of challenges in our healthcare sector management itself. We need to innovate in our own unique way to improve the healthcare coverage without excessive economic burden. Technology such as IT and the mobile phone would be imperative to improving the healthcare situation of the nation.

My co-author, Srijan, has worked on such a technology platform called 'i-Poshan'[21] for improving the coverage and transparency of anganwadis across the nation. Anganwadis are the grassroot-level institutions established by the government to address the issue of malnutrition, mother care and pre-primary education for children below the age of six years. There are over one million anganwadis, each catering to anywhere between 20 and 60 children, providing them free cooked breakfast and lunch, vaccines and basic literacy before they enter school. There are over 2 million field workers working through these anganwadis, who are also responsible for the nutrition of mothers. Overall, anganwadis benefit over 100 million people in the nation, almost on a daily basis. However, anganwadis have also been quoted as centres of 'leakages' and misreporting of attendance. In 'dormant states' such as Uttar Pradesh, Chhattisgarh and Rajasthan, surveys of mothers have reported that only 52% children regularly attended anganwadis — a significant gap compared to the over 90% attendance often reported in the registers filed by anganwadi workers.[22] The gross over-reporting of attendance was also accompanied by 54% of the mothers surveyed in these states reporting that the quantity of food was inadequate — hinting at leakages in the system. On the part of the anganwadi workers, they often complain about the time consumed, up to two hours every day, in filling registers with tedious data and also the delays in payments of their reimbursement claims for items such as fruit and other cooking material — which opens a window for extractive corruption.

The project i-Poshan envisages the use of digital tools and cloud-based computing for connecting anganwadis with centralized monitoring. It is giving a digital device, a low-cost, customized tablet (touchscreen) to every anganwadi worker under the project. The customized software makes it possible for anganwadi workers to operate in local language and on a customized input panel which looks like the current register. This enables them to take attendance, report food stock usage and diseases on the tablet itself.

Using ordinary 2G and 3G technology these tablets are connected on a single cloud-based server—called i-Poshan cloud—where all the data from even far-flung anganwadis is synced regularly. The i-Poshan cloud allows the officials to check any anganwadi's attendance, vaccination, disease reports and food stock on a real-time basis and compare performance indices. Moreover, the i-Poshan cloud would now allow the anganwadi workers to claim reimbursements online using internet banking. It is expected to reduce their claim raise-to-cash receive time from about three months to less than one day. The digital registers help them save time in filling tedious paperwork. Put together, if such a system is implemented across 1 million anganwadis in India, there would be annually a cumulative saving of 730 million man hours and an estimated 6 billion rupees for anganwadi workers by the prevention of loss arising out of delayed payment. It would also be significantly cutting down the misreporting and leakages in the anganwadi system, which is responsible for addressing the acute challenge of malnourishment. It is estimated that malnourishment of children alone causes India a loss of 3% of its GDP, or about the same amount as India spends on its entire healthcare. Even if a small fraction of this loss is plugged by such technological intervention, it would mean the recovery of all investments in it within a year or less.

6

A DIGITALLY EMPOWERED INDIA

India is now being increasingly regarded as amongst the nations benefiting the most from the global digital revolution. India is set for a next generation 'digital revolution' as it implements a $18 billion programme to expand high-speed internet access and offer government services online.[1] As per the communication and IT ministry, the goals 'include broadband internet for 250,000 clusters of villages by 2016 at a cost of about $5.9 billion, cloud storage for citizens and making banking and other data accessible via mobile phones'.[2]

In 2014, when Facebook founder Mark Zuckerberg came to India he made a visit to a village called Chandauli, about 250 kilometres from Delhi. Earlier in 2014, Chandauli got connected to the internet. As a result, hundreds of people—from schoolchildren to seniors—were learning how to use the internet to find information, access government services and connect with their friends and loved ones. This impressed the US business icon so much that he parted with the words, 'Seeing first-hand how people here are using the internet was an incredible experience. One day, if we can connect every village, we can transform many more lives and improve the world for all of us. Chandauli is just the start.' Mark, though well-intentioned, was slightly off the mark. The Indian digital revolution was already well past the first gear and reaching global standards in terms of users and application. Consider this:

- India has over 243 million internet users—giving it the third position in the world only behind China and the US.[3]
- 173 million of these users in India were accessing the Net on mobile devices. The number of rural mobile internet users is about 53 million. The average spend on mobile internet (Rs 235 per month) is nearly half of the expense on mobile connections (Rs 439 per month).[4]
- There are 109 million Indians who are Facebook users, making it the second highest user base, after the US.
- There are about forty million online matrimonial profiles, with thousands of matrimonial sites at combined revenue of over Rs 500 crore. Of course, India is number one in this digital segment.[5]
- Naukri.com, which claims to be 'India's No.1 Job Site', has over 25 million job seekers registered on it and adds 11,000 more every day on its website.
- According to a recent study, young Indian users spend three hours 18 minutes on average every day with their smartphones, of which one-third of the time is spent on apps.
- India's IT exports are almost matching its biggest import—petroleum.

India stands at the tipping point of a digital revolution. Five reasons have propelled India to where it is now on the digital scale, and the promise of an even brighter future outlook.

BACKBONE

The first stage was completed with the Indian telecom industry's efforts which has done a commendable task of providing connectivity of high-speed 3G and now 4G (though with a limited coverage) to even the remoter rural regions of the nation, as we witnessed in interior Badshahpur in Jaunpur (see Prologue). This is what has propelled mobile connectivity to 900 million subscribers—nearby 85% of Indians. In far-flung areas, mobile phone towers are beaming signals on humming diesel generators as they provide connectivity to the people. This is stage one of India's digital revolution, which reached the tipping point by 2010.

THE DIGITAL DEVICE

The second stage of India's digital revolution began with the advent of 'smart phones'. Beginning in the range of Rs 20,000 and upwards in 2008, with a market dominated by the Finnish Nokia, South Korean Samsung and a late, short-lived challenge from Canadian manufacturer Blackberry, smart phones have seen a mega-price war since 2010. Today, the optimally used smart phones, equipped with 3G and camera, are available for as low as Rs 5000. Who was responsible for this price slash? It was not any foreign factor, but a charge of Indian brands which toppled one foreign brand after another. In fact, in 2014 a local Indian brand, Micromax, made ripples across the technology space when it dislodged Samsung as the number one handset seller in India. What's more: Out of the top-five handset sellers in India, three are indigenous companies. The mobile phone price slash could not have come at a more opportune moment for the nation. Desktops and laptops remaining ever so expensive, smart phones quickly became the introduction to the digital arena for the bulk of the nation.

Company	Market share in 2014
Micromax (India)	16.6%
Samsung (South Korea)	14.4%
Nokia (Finland)	10.9%
Karbonn (India)	9.5%
Lava (India)	5.6%

TABLE 1: Market share of major mobile phone manufacturers

THE LANGUAGE GAP

The third leg of the digital revolution almost coincided with the second stage, albeit it went far slower than its predecessor. In a nation with two-thirds literacy spread across two dozen major languages and thousands of dialects, the customization of both input and output is critical to making digital connectivity ubiquitous. However, this revolution is still far from over. The challenge of bridging the language gap in India is twofold. Unlike most Western languages such as English, French, Portuguese, Latin and German, which share identical alpha-numeric characters, nearly all Indian languages use different symbols for their alphabets and numbers. This makes the translation far more difficult. It was finally the advent of Unicode that allowed text and symbols from all of the writing systems of the world to be consistently represented and manipulated by computers. This gave digital devices the ability to enter and read data in many languages. While input-side language barriers have been largely broken, there is much still left on the output side. Automatic translation of web content is still struggling with accuracy and with some of the best institutions from the private and public sectors working on it, we foresee the 'perfect translation code' to be available in two or three years, which can bridge the any-language to any-language gap.

DIGITAL MIGRATION

The fourth stage of the revolution, which is still ongoing, is a 'soft power'—the shift of utilities to digital space. Today, mobile phones are already driving the marketplace in many areas, flattening the space for the smaller and unorganized sectors.

One of the authors[6] who has founded an organization which uses technology for the base of the pyramid came across an interesting case of a vegetable vendor in Delhi, Raghu. Raghu is the regular old-fashioned vegetable vendor, selling produce from a cart he trundles around, similar to over one crore such 'shops on wheels' plying across the streets of the nation. These carts have barely changed in the past six decades in design but the operating model has virtually transformed now. *Raghu is at qualification-level literacy but when one sees him* *'swiping' characters across his touch screen phone, few would believe* *his educational qualification—5th failed . . . twice, before his father* *and his teacher unanimously gave up on his educational career.*

Vegetable vendors like Raghu work on differential pricing, a sort *of commission which they charge on the purchasing price at the* *mandi and the price to the customer. Delhi is filled with many* *mandis, which for a long time had different rates for the same* *vegetables. Hence, it became critical for Raghu and his peers to* *identify the mandi with the lowest price so as to maximize their* *earning. Till 2002, this was a nightmare. When Raghu had to* *replenish his cart, he would have to rely on hearsay from other* *vendors, who in turn relied on an unreliable gossip network to identify* *the best mandi for their purchases. But now, Raghu is able to use a 60* *paisa call to track the vegetable prices halfway across town. Even* *better, he doesn't need to stand calling out to his regular buyers at* *length—he can now give a 'shout' to his customers with a non-* *chargeable missed call. One estimate by experts is, that a regular* *vegetable vendor in the streets of Delhi saves up to 33% of his time* *and 25% of his cost of operation by using his mobile phone—the* *frontline gadget of India's digital mission.*

*

This is the 21st century digital migration of India, it affects the organized and unorganized sector equally. Today, at least 100 Indian cities have GPS-enabled cabs which can be booked over mobile applications with a touch or two of the screen. Governments no longer boast of e-governance—that is obsolete—they now speak of m-governance, or mobile governance. A nation who many believed had a culture of two hours of bargaining for a two-hundred-rupee worth of buying is now teeming with customers buying in seconds from e-stores trusting a set of two or three photographs shown on their mobile screens. India's current e-commerce market, based on digital devices, has an annual revenue of $11 billion—of which $8 billion is e-travel, a market which has matured faster than the rest. The much talked-about e-retail was worth about $3 billion only. But if experts are to be believed, and India goes the way of China, the Indian internet market is set to rise from $11 billion in 2013 to $137 billion by 2020.[7] In the same time, the market capitalization of these internet businesses could touch $160–200 billion from the present $4 billion.[8] The reliance and trust on digital application is so deep rooted that when a popular taxi-booking site decided to play an April Fool prank in 2015, claiming to start a new helicopter taxi service at Rs 499 per hour, most people readily believed the announcement and it took days for popular social media to come to terms with the fact it was a joke.

THE NEW DEMAND

It does not end here, not yet. We see the Digital India Revolution going much further. With awareness and access, there will be a surge for more—when people will ask, 'Why not 100% digital?' and 'Why not we get all information online, why not all payments online?' As a nation challenged with scarcity, from teachers to doctors, from judges to policemen, a 100% digital regime can be an answer—the leapfrogging way to many of our acute issues—which hitherto seemed unsolvable on the sheer scale problem. Digital demand gives the voiceless an opportunity to obtain political accountability and economic inclusion, a chance at social mobility, and such a demand is bound to gather democratic momentum. For instance, the 2015 Delhi state elections saw all three major political parties promising free or heavily subsidized wireless internet for all citizens. Similarly, in 2014, the Central government decided to go online with the daily attendance level of all its departments. Backed with a biometric tracking mechanism and a real-time website updation, the portal attendancegov.in shows the in–out times for all departments down to the last detail. Two years before this, in 2012, the elections in India's largest state (by population), Uttar Pradesh, were comprehensively won by a political party which promised free laptops and tablets to all the students of the state. Digital inclusion is the next democratic slogan.

We see this as the new momentum which will only go forward. There will be added demand for higher scale, more scope and better quality of digital services. Digital will be the next economic engine too. NASSCOM reports that India's IT exports in 2014–15 would reach $99 billion, up from less than $50 billion in 2011.[9] With India's oil import bill expected at $100 billion in 2014–15,[10] the India IT workforce, manned by no more than 3 million people,[11] is creating enough export to write-off the entire oil import bill of the nation of 1.2 billion.

We will now build further on this 'new demand', and later in this chapter, we will be analysing the opportunities, challenges and future map of the Digital India.

India is the world's largest sourcing destination for the IT industry, accounting for approximately 52% of the $124–130 billion market. The industry employs about 10 million Indians.[12]

*

STOPGAPS AND LEAPFROGS

There are two innovations which can be done to any public system delivery. One is to meet immediate necessity—we call it the Stopgap Measure—and the other is to create a more feasible and optimal futuristic reform. We call it the Leapfrog. While neither is preferable to the other, it must be understood that often they work best in tandem.

Stopgaps are innovations, often short-lived, which are implemented to meet the urgent necessities of today, for which a nation or system cannot wait for a long-term solution to emerge. They are often much needed 'Band-Aid' measures, used to minimize losses and temporarily augment services.

Leapfrogs are long-term innovations, carefully planned by keeping the ecosystem and alternatives in mind. They often have the tendency to skip intermediary steps to adapt to a new ecosystem of the future, as for instance when India leapfrogged in telecom by skipping the stage of wired telephone lines and landing straight into nationwide mobile telephony. Leapfrogging is long-term optimization.

IT and IT-enabled services offer a chance at both stopgaps and leapfrogs.

Let us take an example of this, in the Digital India context. India currently has a doctor-to-people ratio of 0.7:1000, which means 0.70 doctors for every 1000 people. In Norway the ratio is above 4.3. Most of the healthier ratios are upwards of 2.5. Now it is amply clear that India's current healthcare system is ailing and wants urgent action as under the current 0.70 ratio essential services are suffering. However, at the same time, it is nearly impossible to aim for improving the doctor-to-people ratio to 4.3 or even 3.3 given the size of the population. Hence, we need to innovate a better model for future expansion where even with lesser and more feasible ratio of between 2 and 2.5; we can achieve the same service levels as other advanced healthcare nations. This requires leapfrog interventions.

Rapidly connecting rural health centres and health workers with simple diagnostics can perhaps be a stopgap. Training new rural doctors conversant with digital technologies and telemedicine to reduce the travel distances and enable better utilization of existing and new doctors would be the leapfrog. Of course, as with all leapfrogs, this assumes that the eco-system will evolve in the next few years to enable such a system.

*

The land area of India is around 3.3 million square kilometres with 7000 kilometres of coastline. The area encompasses deserts, hilltops, mountains, seashores, islands, valleys and plains. Out of the billion plus population in the country, 70% live in 600,000 villages. We are in the process of a societal transformation towards sustainable development for our growth. This we propose to realize in a time-bound manner by promoting a knowledge society for empowering the entire nation. Electronic and knowledge connectivity is the key to realize this goal. Connecting a billion people poses multiple challenges and also unleashes a whole lot of opportunities. In this situation Digital India can provide a number of leapfrogs and stop-gaps through a network of cloud-based data, processing and knowledge. What could these be?

1. National Citizen Database Cloud

Backed with Aadhaar, or Biometric Universal ID for citizens, there is an opportunity to create a comprehensive database service for all the citizens. Such a database can go beyond citizen identification and can take the role of a single cloud to maintain records related to health parameters, education, skills and financial inclusion for individual citizens. In a scenario where a majority of citizens are using mobile phone, such a cloud should be accessible via mobile phone — even for those without internet support, using Voice-Based Response System.

2. National e-Health Cloud

India has 0.7 physicians and 0.7 hospital beds per 1000 people. As shown in the comparative table, these are both well below the international averages. Of course, as pointed out earlier in the book, we need significant private and public investment in improving these benchmarks to bring in international standards in our healthcare. Such a transformation will indeed be costly and time consuming. But digital connectivity can be a leapfrogging winner here too. At least as a stopgap.

Country	Number of physicians per 1000 population[13]	Number of hospital beds per 1000 population[14]
Brazil	1.9	2.3
China	1.9	3.8
USA	2.5	2.9
Norway	4.3	3.3
Singapore	2.0	2.0
South Korea	2.1	N/A
Sri Lanka	0.7	3.6
India	0.7	0.7

TABLE 2: Health infrastructure in different countries

With the increasing penetration of internet and the mobile phone in the remoter areas it is becoming a feasible opportunity to use e-Healthcare and m-Healthcare, using telemedicine, remote diagnosis and online ordering of drugs. This can be coupled with an aggressive preventive healthcare regime to drastically bring down the disease incidence by combating it with information and knowledge, besides just medicine.

Barefoot Doctors: The Community-Owned National Health Care Movement in China

'Barefoot Doctors' is a part of the Chinese Rural Health Care Movement which began in the 1950s and gathered momentum after 1968. The Barefoot Doctors were essentially farmers who were given about six months of basic medical and paramedical training in a hospital and then sent back to their villages to farm and also to provide basic medical care to the people. Their training focused largely on preventive health care, prevention of epidemics, and diseases specifically pertaining to their region.

Each barefoot doctor was provided with a set of 40–50 Western and Chinese medicines for dispensing as required.

They helped with immunizations, childbirth, and improvement of sanitation. Each barefoot doctor had the option of training local youths as village health aides, who would work on a specific type of disease. Typically, a barefoot doctor would dedicate about half of his or her time towards agriculture and the other half in providing health care.

The barefoot doctors were paid out of a collective welfare fund from local farmers' contributions. They earned about half as much as a fully trained doctor. They provided healthcare to the people at the grassroots level. They would attend to about 15 patients a day, and make 150 home visits a month. In about 75–90% of the cases, the problems would be solved locally, and for the remaining, the patients would be referred to a hospital.

This mission, under a rural cooperative medical system, at its peak, covered about 90% of China's villages. The barefoot doctors were at the forefront of the Chinese rural healthcare mission till the 1980s. The impact of this movement was reflected in the healthcare system of the nation and set the foundation for a healthy and economically progressive society.

During the era of the barefoot doctors, the average life expectancy in China almost doubled, from 35 years in 1965 to 68.9 in the early 1980s, The infant mortality rate fell, from 200 at the start of 1950, to below 30 per 1,000 live births in the early 1980s.

The success of the barefoot doctors in the healthcare system is attributed largely to the fact that the movement was essentially a community-owned, community-trained and community-benefitting model. The fact that they were mainly farmers made them more approachable and fostered a feeling of trust. Since they lived in the same village, they were also available for consultation 24x7 and, therefore, were further relied on by the people.

Post-1980s, the barefoot doctors were permitted to take a medical examination and, subject to it, they were reorganized as village doctors, healthcare workers and licensed assistant

doctors. Today, China's villages have more than 880,000
rural doctors, about 110,000 licensed assistant doctors and
50,000 health workers.

(Adapted from the authors' book *Target 3 Billion*)

For such a mission to be successful we need an extensive
support system for e-Health initiatives. Telemedicine has been
fairly successful in many places in the nation and such models
need to be replicated. A specialized department for e-Health and
m-Health needs to be formulated in a mission mode method as an
intersection of IT and health ministries. There are over 23,000
Primary Healthcare Centres across the nation. Each of these can
be a centre for delivering the e-Preventive Health, e-Diagnosis and
Telemedicine. From 2005 onwards, the Ministry of Health and
Family Welfare (MoHFW) has started the Accredited Social Health
Activists (ASHAs) programme to enable use of paid community
health workers under the National Rural Health Mission (NRHM).
The total number of ASHA workers in India was reported in July
2013 to be 870,089; evidently all of them are women. Can these
ASHA workers, spread across almost every single village in the
nation, become the agents for delivering the first level of e-Health?
Using simple devices, such as touchscreen phones, available for as
low as Rs 4000, loaded with some well-designed 'mobile apps' and
plug-in tools, can these 800,000-plus educated and reasonably
trained workers be deployed in the additional role of on-spot e-
diagnosis and simple treatment in the same model as the Barefoot
doctors were used in China?

We believe that a combination of the physical assets (such as
PHCs) and human resource (such as ASHA) can be streamlined
into a well thought-out national e-Health cloud connecting the
healthcare parameters of all citizens. This cloud can lead to lesser
diseases, predictable disease combating and cheaper diagnosis,
and enable the specialist to connect to the needy—despite being
separated by physical distances. It can eventually lead to a better

utilization of our overstretched health assets such as hospitals and physicians and provide breathing space and optimization to the healthcare sector.

3. National Open Source Education Cloud

We had discussed earlier about the poor performance of our students in the Programme for International Student Assessment (PISA) survey for reading, mathematics and science. In addition to the suggestions already mentioned, Digital India can go a long way in helping improve India's education. How? We recommend a National Open Source Education Cloud—which caters to the needs of three segments. First, the students, especially those below 18 years of age, who are in school or preparing for competitive examinations. Second, for teachers of these students. Third, for higher level learning and university professors. And fourth, for skill development and adult education in specific fields—especially those related to entrepreneurship and better income generation.

Teachers of the nation need to be well connected to enable a knowledge sharing environment.

A worthy example in this direction is the initiative Share My Lesson started in 2012 to enable teachers from all across the world, especially the US, to share their innovative methods of teaching basic subjects. Till date, it has over 262,000 learning resources, all contributed freely by teachers and available at no charge as open source to a general audience. It was seeded when the American Federation of Teachers partnered with Britain's TES Connect to build the largest online community for US teachers to collaborate and share teaching resources and innovative ideas. The announcement about Share My Lesson was made on 19 June 2012, at the Global Education Conference at Stanford University. The AFT and TES Global (the owners of the TES) are investing $10 million to develop the site.[15]

Such a large-scale, open source, learning tool sharing platform can also be envisaged as part of Digital India and its e-learning component. Moreover, a significant additional step would be to ensure language interoperability, with translation of the best learning tools contributed in all major languages.

We also need to work on using the National Open Source Education Cloud for up-skilling and reskilling workers. In a changing ecosystem new technologies and skills are being created rapidly and old knowledge is rendered meaningless. In such a scenario, the National Open Source Education Cloud can be the one-stop solution for identifying lessons for specific occupation groups drawn from the Citizen Database. These lessons can be best shaped as electronic- and mobile-based plans available under a common cloud. In fact, towards the end of 2014, a well-known Indian mobile company shifted its marketing campaign to mobile-based learning—encouraging self-training by using their mobile network. While, the campaign, titled IIN,[16] showcasing how a mobile-based 'institution' could become the saviour for those who were denied mainstream education, was met with mixed reaction, it did highlight that in the coming times digital-connectivity-based companies will see a major foothold in the education sector. It has been widely reported that the Government of India plans to provide free Wi-Fi in 250,000 schools and all universities—and such an e-learning can be integrated with such a hardware system.

4. Indian Regional Navigation Satellite System (IRNSS)

IRNSS is an indigenous alternative to the well-known Global Positioning System, or GPS. Expected to be completed in 2016 by ISRO, it has an interesting history beginning at the end of the last century.

The year 1999 was a very eventful one for India. It was the year when there was an unprovoked infiltration by Pakistani troops, who crossed the Line of Control in Jammu and Kashmir leading to a mountain war between the two nuclear powers. When we first tracked Pakistani troops who had taken positions in India's territory in Kargil, one of the first things the Indian military sought was GPS data for the region. The space-based navigation system maintained by the US government would have provided vital information to us. But to our disappointment the US denied it to us. While it put us in difficulty, it also made us realize the need for an indigenous satellite navigation system. It took more than a decade to master this system. The accurate positioning of ground using a satellite is a complex task, requiring multiple geosynchronous satellites that work in close tandem with each other; ground-based ranging station and the main ground station—which is currently located in Byalalu in Karnataka. A goal of complete Indian control has been stated, with the space segment, ground segment and user receivers all to be built in India. The total cost of this project is Rs 1420 crore or about $223 million,[17] compared to the cost of GPS, which is over eleven times, at $2.5 billion.[18] There will be a total of seven satellites to be placed in the geosynchronous orbit for completing this system—IRNSS-1A to IRNSS-1G. As on 28 March 2015, four satellites have been successfully placed and another three remain to be launched—it is expected that this unique navigational project will be completed by 2016.

Such an alternative navigation system to GPS not only has a strategic and military use but also tremendous civilian application. The cost of this system would make it very cost competitive, and open many new vistas for income creation—such as logistics, security, agriculture, land mapping and mining. In a technological transformation, where even three-wheeler autos are now being fitted with navigation systems, the IRNSS can be a potent tool in the hands of the people to create many new enterprises around.

5. National Financial Services Cloud

India has seen an unprecedented spike in the number of bank account holders as the result of a governmental thrust for financial inclusion, which eventually culminated in the Pradhan Mantri Jan Dhan Yojana (PMJDY) in 2014. The PMJDY itself saw the opening of 115 million accounts in less than one year.[19]

A similar thrust was also undertaken in China. In fact, both China and India saw strong growth in account ownership between 2011 and 2014—in China account penetration increased from 64% to 79%, and in India from 35% to 53%.[20]

But some critical issues still remain between now and our target to achieve full-scale financial inclusion. First, while accounts were opened under a concerted effort, only a few of them are actually being used. For instance, only 28% of Jan Dhan Yojana accounts are currently active and the majority are zero balance accounts. Second, 90% of the total retail transactions in India are settled in cash. One primary reason is that the Indian retail sector is heavily fragmented—with about 8.5 million retail outlets who do not see efficacy in the current model of electronic payment because of their smaller scale. No wonder, ATMs were used to withdraw cash worth Rs 20 trillion in 2014. Where can Digital India help to overcome such problems? We recommend this through the National Financial Cloud.

M-PESA Revolutionizing the Banking World

Underdeveloped and developing countries face a chronic problem of under-banked population. Over the years, various physical and digital interventions have tried to address this issue but none of them has been as effective and successful as M-PESA. M-PESA has been able to bring a revolution in the banking world. It was initiated by a micro-finance company to facilitate repayments, especially among the marginalized sections of the population. Later on, it was taken by Safaricom, a subsidiary of telecom behemoth Vodafone. This move helped in expanding the scope for M-PESA services to be provided to a larger section of the customers.

The process of using M-PESA is extremely simple and easy to understand. The process is as follows:

1. **Registration:** Any person who wants to avail the services has to get registered with the company Safaricom. The

company provides the customer with a SIM card. This SIM card has the M-PESA application loaded on it.

2. **Security:** The most significant aspect related to a person's bank account is its security. The customer needs to create a PIN for the security of the account. Generally, such a PIN is a four-digit number.

3. **Receiving and Withdrawing Money:** M-PESA allows receiving and withdrawal of cash from this account. This is made possible via the retailers of the company (Safaricom) and other related retailers.

Salient Features of M-PESA

- The average **amount of transaction value** is between $20-30.

- Average **number of transactions** in a quarter ranges from 20 to 25.

- Money from M-PESA **can be sent to any person** who may/may not be an M-PESA account holder.

- Money received can be kept in the mobile or can be withdrawn from the authorized agent by the recipient.

- Various **Central Banks** across the globe have been **supporting this initiative** as it helps them in achieving their goal of universal banking of the population, e.g. **Bank of Kenya**.

In a nutshell, the National Financial Cloud would have to focus on how to integrate banking with digital inclusion through mobile phones and low-cost internet to the last mile. It should be able to identify and deliver area and economic class-wise customized financial products, loans, saving instruments and insurance. For this purpose it needs to integrate with other citizens databases such as Citizen Cloud. The National Financial Cloud would enable new tools for promoting e-cash such as mobile money and pre-paid instruments. Pre-paid instruments (PPI) are widely regarded as friendlier to the lower economic group and easier to use in a fragmented retail market such as that of India. However, the current gains have been in the more traditional and top-end serving financial instruments. For instance, as per the Reserve Bank of India, in 2014 there were 394 million debit cards, 19 million credit cards, 160,000 ATMs and one million Point of Sale devices (basically swipe machines). PPIs were hardly a significant number and served only about Rs 81 billion of the annual transactions.[21] The National Financial Cloud needs to encourage these new and more inclusive financial tools in the form of pre-paid instruments. Another area which the National Financial Cloud needs to focus on would be in the area of mobile-based banking, including customer-to-merchant transfers via simple mobile phones using PIN authentication such as that used by M-PESA.

There is another critical application of the National Financial Services Cloud—replacing paper money with electronic cash. This electronic cash or digital money can go a long way in addressing the issue of corruption in the nation. The size of the black economy in India is about Rs 25 lakh crore, or 40% of the total GDP.[22] Furthermore, India loses about Rs 10 lakh crore every year to illegal activities, including fake products, pirated goods, illegal trades, bribery, gambling and a host of unaccounted activities which are solely done on cash basis.[23] In 2011, a government report claimed that four out of every 1000 currency notes in circulation in India are fake, casting a serious doubt on the 'credibility of the rupee as a legal tender'.[24] Another major sector plagued with black money is real estate, where between 20% and 50% of the payment is typically done in cash and completely unaccounted for. Builders often refer to this as the 'cash–cheque ratio'.

Can we solve these issues plaguing our economy with the replacement of paper notes with electronic money? We believe it is possible. Even if done for high-value notes, it is a digital solution to India's multiple problems of corruption, illegal trades and counterfeit notes. This has to come as a combination of Point of Sale devices, debit cards and mobile money transactions.

The greatest challenge will be in the retail sector, which is 92% unorganized in India. In 2013-14, the total size of the retail sector in India was about Rs 31 trillion ($534 billion).[25] Out of this, the organized sector was only about Rs 2.4 trillion. There are over 14 million outlets operating in the country and only 4% of them are larger than 500 sq. ft in size.[26] Thus, the real challenge would be to bring the other 96% shops, all small sized, and many in rural areas, into the digital payment bracket. This is where mobile money transfer can play a very important role—similar to the transactions we highlighted in Jaunpur in the prologue. To complete the picture, we would also recommend the creation of a new mobile money bank, dedicated solely to completing mobile transactions and developing expertise in it.

6. India E-Commerce Cloud

India is being discussed as the fastest growing e-commerce market in the world. From cars to books and from clothes to travel everything is now available online—and the Indian customer is responding well to it. While e-commerce is relatively cost effective, for sheer technical complications, it still remains beyond the reach of many smaller business, handicraft makers, farmers and local products and foods. Digital India should focus on creating a plug-in cloud for e-commerce on a national scale. We call it the India E-Com Cloud. Such an e-com cloud should have provision for integrating business-to-consumer, consumer-to-consumer and business-to-business sales. It can be a conglomeration of the existing e-commerce operators and customized for easier access to small sellers, especially in rural areas, who can access the vast international market through such a cloud which can synchronize with a mobile.

A noteworthy example in this area is Alibaba.com, a Chinese company, which is the largest e-commerce web portal in the world and valued at over $231 billion. Started in 1998 by Jack Ma and seventeen other founders, the group's websites accounted for over 60% of the parcels delivered in China by March 2013, and 80% of the nation's online sales by September 2014.[27] Alibaba has become so large that its portals sold good worth more than $170 billion per year, more than the two next biggest companies, Amazon and eBay, put together.[28] Alibaba.com handles sales between importers and exporters from more than 240 countries and regions making it an incredible asset in improving China's trade ties and boosting its exports. These figures explain why Harvard's William Kirby, an expert on Chinese business, calls Alibaba a transformative firm—'a private company that has done more for China's national economy than most state-owned enterprises.'[29]

7. National Judicial Cloud

At the end of 2013, there were 31,367,915 open cases working their way through the system, from the lowest chambers at district levels to the Supreme Court.[30] According to Bloomberg *Businessweek* calculations, 'If the nation's judges attacked their backlog nonstop— with no breaks for eating or sleeping—and closed 100 cases every hour, it would take more than thirty-five years to catch up.' Statistics speak for it. India had only 15.5 judges for every million people in 2013, then prime minister Manmohan Singh said at the time. The US has more than 100 judges for every million.[31] Can Digital India enable a National Judicial Cloud to enable timely and quality justice to all its citizens? We believe it can.

This can be done at two levels. First, through complete digitalization and online availability of case documents and proceedings which will eliminate the intermediary processes. And second, by video conferencing of cases through regularly available internet tools. Computer-based analytical advisory for judges and lawyers can be instrumental in speeding up the judicial system and also make it easier and cost-effective for citizens.

8. India Innovation Cloud (IIC)

India is a land of innovations. Some of these are on shop floors, some in laboratories, some in colleges and some in plain huts and farms in the form of grassroot innovations. We propose a National Innovation Cloud under the Digital India umbrella which can be a seamless and freely accessible database to upload and download innovations, and a processing platform to judge the efficacy and performance of innovations in the pipeline with cloud-based help in designing, materials, mechanical parameters and structural performance. IIC would thus help develop innovations into viable systems and products that can be taken up on a large scale.

9. National Security and Disaster Management Cloud

Of course, a very important consequence of a digitalized India would be its help in disaster management and security. Weather data and warnings could be extensively available to all, from fisherman to farmer, to help them plan better. With increasingly digitalized security, including video cameras in public places and other modern tools, a single cloud of all security-related data collected from public and private sources can be managed under an authority such as the National Investigation Agency (NIA). An important element in this cloud would be keeping an eye on cyber security of public and private data and websites.

There are undoubtedly many critical challenges to overcome before Digital India can truly become inclusive. For instance, the average bandwidth capacity in developing countries for every 10,000 people is 28 mbps. In India, it is still around 6 mbps. More and more people need to be given digital literacy beyond just the basics. Panchayats need to be enabled and encouraged to make digital tools as their mainstay. Digital literacy teachers and IT syllabi need to be created for thousands of schools, who are already struggling with their conventional syllabus.

7

CREATING A 21st CENTURY POLITICAL SYSTEM AND GOVERNANCE OF ETHICS AND EFFICIENCY

At the stroke of midnight on 15 August 1947, humanity witnessed the birth of the largest democracy ever to exist. While the first Prime Minister of India, Pandit Nehru, spoke about India's tryst with destiny and unfurled the tricolour in the capital Delhi, while the crowds rejoiced as the world watched, people wondered and questioned, where was the architect of Indian freedom—Mahatma Gandhi?

On the eve of independence, Mahatma Gandhi chose to remain in Calcutta healing hearts and bringing harmony and peace between the Hindu and Muslim communities of Bengal. *The Collected Works* of Mahatma Gandhi narrate how the Father of the Nation spent his day on the momentous occasion. One of several meetings Gandhiji had on 15 August at his temporary home in Beliaghata (Kolkata) was with the ministers of the newly installed government of West Bengal. When the ministers sought his blessings, Gandhiji told them,

'Today, you have worn on your heads a crown of thorns. The seat of power is a nasty thing. You have to remain ever wakeful on that seat. You have to be more truthful, more non-violent, more

Dr Kalam would often stop at roadside dhabas to have chai on his journeys into India's heartland. He was keen to understand how the local economy operated and how the youth could be turned into entrepreneurs. Here he is seen with Srijan Pal Singh at one such stop they made in Moradabad, Uttar Pradesh. Dr Kalam looks back at his convoy of police officers and asks them to join in as tea is served.

Dr Kalam with Dhanshyam Sharma (right), his personal assistant, and Srijan. He later sat down with the owner of the tea stall and offered suggestions on how to improve his business.

Dr Kalam makes an entrance at his IIM Shillong class in 2014. He visited the campus every year and took a three-day course on a topic of contemporary relevance.

Dr Kalam takes a question from a student at his 2014 IIM Shillong class, where the theme was 'Global Vision 2030', as Srijan looks on.

Dr Kalam took great pride in his role as a teacher. Here he is seen writing on the blackboard during a visit to a school in Tamil Nadu.

Dr Kalam at the centre of the 2014 IIM Shillong class photo.

Dr Kalam believed that India's greatest potential and untapped advantage are its villages, and he was a proponent of PURA—Providing Urban Amenities in Rural Areas. Here he is seen addressing 40,000 children in Loni, Maharashtra, a shining example of PURA.

Dr Kalam waves at a large crowd on the ground as his chopper lands in Kannauj, Uttar Pradesh, on 8 July 2015, a few weeks before he passed away. There he inaugurated a mini solar plant grid to provide clean power to distant villages.

humble and more forbearing. You had been put to test during the British regime. But in a way it was no test at all. But now there will be no end to your being tested. Do not fall a prey to the lure of wealth. May God help you! You are there to serve the villages and the poor.'

Gandhiji's advice and caution are still relevant today, even after over six decades of freedom. It is a question every citizen and leader of the nation needs to ask himself—How far have we succeeded or failed in the 'test' Gandhiji referred to and how much has the leadership, especially the political leadership, been immune to the lure of wealth?

The common man's perception of the political system of the nation has been usually far from satisfactory. The problem is reflected in many independent assessments including that by Transparency International, which ranked India at 85 in its list of most corrupt nations in 2014–15.[1] Though we must also state that this ranking has improved from the previous year, when India hit the 95th position. The negative image is also reflected in the international bribe-payers index, where 25% of the respondents, who were senior multinational businessmen, indicated that 'Bribery to High-Ranking Politician or Political Parties' is a prevalent form of foreign bribery.

This perception placed Indian Political Corruption third on the list, where it is surpassed only by two other nations in the survey— Russia and Mexico. There are many reasons for such a downslide in national politics over the past six decades.

First, the last two decades have seen the ushering in of a new phase in the economy of the nation. Pre-liberalization, with the tight control over assets and procedures, the stakes were much lower and while the instances of corruption were aplenty, the quantum of each case was limited. With the new liberalized economy, coupled with galloping technological progress, the spectrum of assets coming out of controlled licensing is significantly coming down. For instance, back in the 1970s, who would have ever imagined that in another three decades national assets like mines, petroleum reserves, forests and telecom bandwidth would be worth billions of dollars to the industries across the world. The recent discoveries of new assets and advent of better technologies to process these assets into meaningful economic returns has also propelled the stakes involved in corruption to levels higher than ever imagined.

Secondly, there is a distinct feeling that politics is fast evolving into a game of musical chairs where the same set of leaders, or their favoured few, occupy the seats of power with huge entry barriers for others. Where this set of leaders lacks integrity, the baton passes from one corrupt leader to another who is part of this set. Politics needs streamlined processes for the people to pluck out and permanently discard the corrupted and also a mechanism by which fresh talent and creative leaders can find their way into the system, using ethical means.

Third, election processes have become extremely expensive for political parties, both national and state. The proliferation of parties has significantly added to the burden of elections on the nation, and also distorted the political equations post elections, leading to the spread of corruption.

The debauchery of the political leaders perhaps hurts the citizens more than any other form of corruption. The greatest tool which democracies give to their citizen is the power to vote. This entitlement of an equal vote remains the most cherished right, especially to those who are at the bottom of the pyramid. For them the vote remains the foremost opportunity to be heard and holds the promise for enabling a turnaround which they can be witness to within their lifetime. The vote is a symbol of the voter's unflinching faith in democracy, the system and the leaders who stand up for election. When the leadership turns indifferent, corrupt or callous, it is a breach of faith and a shattering of hope.

But apathy and indifference was never, and will never be, an answer. It is not difficult to fathom that political corruption is easily the most dangerous of all forms. In any mature or emerging democracy, the quality of the political leadership can mean the difference between a welfare state and a bankrupt one. This concept is not limited to India alone, but pervasive across the globe. Figure 1 shows examples of how degraded political leadership devastated national economies. It also shows how a corrupt leadership, given opportunity by an indifferent citizenry, pushed back the economic and social progress of a nation by decades.

There is a brighter side too. First, while the fact that over time our political system has seen ethical decay is undisputed, yet there are ample of cases where political leadership has shown the capability and resolve to combat the menace of inefficiency and corruption.

In December 2008, the speaker of the newly elected Karnataka Legislative Assembly invited me to conduct an orientation programme for the members of the assembly and council. The programme was held on 13 December 2008, in the beautiful campus of the Indian Institute of Management, Bangalore and attended by all the members, including the chief minister. A few weeks before the class, I decided to send the members a set of questions (shown in the box) pertaining to their constituency and its development. The questions were by no means easy. They were diverse, and answering them required a sound understanding of the constituency and its profile and a keen interest in finding an optimal mix of societal action, technological innovation and management of the available resources. I was uncertain but hopeful of receiving responses to the question; it was a hope which I and my team had decided to put to test. To my pleasant surprise, 66 members sent me well thought-out answers. We went through each answer carefully, and it was a happy experience to find that most of the answers were innovative, precise and contained an implementation plan. They reflected soundness of ideas and thoroughness of analysis. I had responses ranging from octogenarian MLAs to young first-timers. I discussed many of the ideas in the

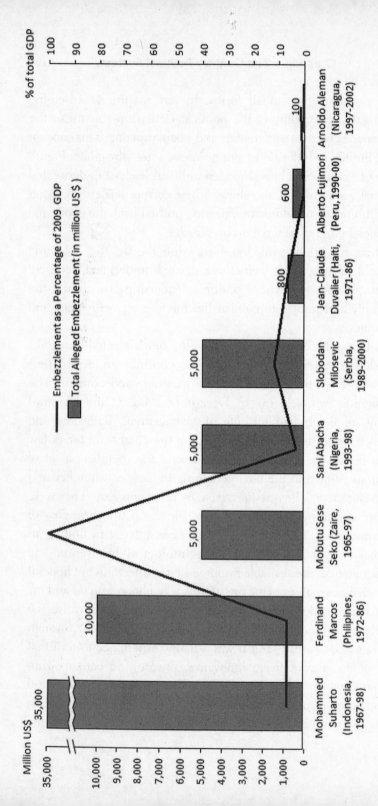

FIGURE 1: Alleged political corruption worldwide and its impact on the nations

orientation sessions, and the members received them with absorbed attention. My interaction with the MLAs and MLCs was followed by many interesting and pertinent questions from the members which brought forth issues and ideas which need attention.

Questions to the MLAs and MLCs of the Karnataka Assembly, 2008

1. What change would you bring in your constituency (name) after 2.5 years and later after 5 years?

2. Do you have plans to realize 100% literacy in your constituency? If so, you may indicate your plan?

3. With what skill and expertise will you empower the members of your constituency to increase the per capita income by at least two times?

4. Will you have a plan to plant at least 100,000 trees in your constituencies?

5. Would you like to get all the water bodies in your constituencies rejuvenated after desilting and activation of inlet and outlet?

6. Would you like to get sanitary facility in every home of your constituency with adequate water supply and its management?

7. Will you plan for your constituency multi-cropping and also plantation of jatropha (a bio-fuel generating plant) in wasteland?

8. Will you make your constituency free from power cuts and power shortage using renewable energy sources?

9. Will you pave the way for peaceful and prosperous living of the citizens in your constituency?

The Karnataka assembly orientation experience also changed my own impressions. The youthful enthusiasm, in an open, candid democratic setup, which many of the members exhibited, showed that sincere leadership and innovation hold the key to a successful political system. Each of the 66 MLAs was capable of achieving monumental transformation in their constituencies. If we could inject many such talented representatives into our system, if we could provide the necessary framework and support to the existing innovative ideas in governance, and, above all, if all this could be done in a way which is underpinned by ethics and a value system, a truly great system of governance would be achieved. The legislature is the most empowered body with resources at its disposal to effect change at far greater pace and extent than any other body. If political systems could be reformed to a dynamic and zero-corruption body, the ramifications of the change would soon be pervasive across the institutions and society.

At the heart of creating a political system which is corruption-free also resides the quest to create a system which is truly responsive to its citizens, a vibrant system where politics becomes a means of service to the people rather than a saddle of governance. A corruption-free political system would give opportunity to that which represents innovation and ideas, than emerge as a safehouse for the archaic and morally dilapidated. It would be a system which would attract bright young minds and emerge as a career to which parents would feel proud to send their children. It would be a system where the upright and talented could work with integrity and succeed with integrity.

A strategic approach towards building a more resilient and corruption-free system would incorporate a variety of issues and aspects. These would include:

- Introduction of reforms in the election process of the nation to present a wider and more powerful array of choices to the common man
- Facilitation of processes to realistically bring down the election expenses and thereby also bring down the entry cost into politics
- Making politics a viable career option for the best talent in

governance which exists in the nation, especially amongst the women and youth

- Ensuring politics and politicians are always on the learning curve, with a focus on developmental politics, and accountability for the welfare promised and delivery on the promises made.

'How can this be realized?'

The most critical process in a political system is elections. The colossal truth of any democracy is that the ultimate fate of who will be in power and who will not is invariably dependent on the process and outcome of the elections. Elections are the opportunity for people to make choices based on their concerns.

Oath given to the Legislators of the Karnataka Assembly, 2008

1. I am proud of being a member of the Legislative Assembly/Council of Karnataka of high tradition.

2. Welfare and happiness of the citizens of my constituency comes first always and every time.

3. I will work and work to make my constituency fully literate, healthy, empowered, happy and poverty free before 2013.

4. I will celebrate the success of the citizens of my constituency.

5. My constituency is my life and my state and the nation is my soul.

6. I will not allow any discrimination in my constituency by way of religion, language, caste or creed.

7. I will be transparent in all my actions and become a role model for all the citizens of my constituency. I will work with integrity and succeed with integrity.

Here, I recall a question raised at the Karnataka Assembly Orientation Session at IIM Bangalore. At the end of the session, I administered the members an oath with seven points. The members enthusiastically repeated the oath after me. The last line of the oath read 'I will work with integrity, and succeed with integrity.' After completing his oath, one young legislator rose up and boldly asked me a question which reflected the harsh reality of our electoral process, 'Mr Kalam, you have asked all of us to take an oath of working with integrity and to be transparent. How is this possible? Do you know how much I had to spend in the elections?' The hall fell silent. The words of the legislator perhaps echoed in most of the members present there. The young member continued, 'I spent at least Rs 80 lakh on my election. There was no other option as each opponent was doing the same. To garner the money I had to mortgage much of my property and jewellery of my wife. How can I work with integrity and succeed with integrity in such a situation, please tell me.'

I had the chief minister and the speaker of the House by my side. I looked at them; we were all puzzled—there was no answer I could give—the question pointed to the need for a systemic reform.

The words of the young legislator are re-affirmed by various sources. Elections have become an increasingly cost-intensive proposition and an outlet for black money. The cost of Lok Sabha elections in 2009 was over Rs 30,000 crore (Rs 300 billion). Out of this, only about 20% was official spending by the Election Commission and the state and central governments. This is, of course, far higher than the stipulated ceiling on expense as per election rules.

Success in politics should be an outcome of the capability to lead and deliver, not of expense.

Thus bringing down the cost of elections in a realistic manner and ensuring accountability of spending is paramount to not only nip corruption at the bud, but also to make politics healthy and attractive for talented youth again.

Let us come back to the question at the Karnataka assembly on how politicians can work with integrity and succeed with integrity, in a scenario when the cost of elections is so astronomical. We hinted that the solution lies in systemic reform. One such system I and my team suggested at the orientation class was the possibility of 'state-sponsored elections'. Under a state-sponsored election the Election Commission with a network of other competent bodies would completely take care of all the election expenses of the candidates. Questions followed. Would all the candidates be given sponsorship? If that was the case, then the cost of sponsorship would be exceedingly high given the large number of candidates? If only a certain number of candidates were sponsored, then what would be the basis of their selection?

The most plausible solution would be the one which gives every candidate a fair chance and yet is economically feasible to undertake. It should also inherently discourage unserious candidates from contesting. Let us call this a 'Conditionally and Accountably Sponsored System of Elections'. This would have three important aspects:

a) Sponsored Elections: Under this system, every candidate contesting would be allotted a fixed account with the Election Commission or its associated body and the government would take care of the entire election expense of all the candidates. The sum to be allotted to each of the candidates, say T, would be a sum of two amounts—first, a fixed base amount equal for each constituency, say B, and then another variable amount (V), which would be a function of the cost of campaigning in the local conditions, size of the constituency and its terrain. Of course, within a constituency, the total allocation $(T = B + V)$ would be similar for each of the candidates. This amount would also include any party contribution or activities sponsored by any political party.

b) Conditional Sponsorship: Sponsorship would come with one significant pre-condition. While the state would readily take care of the cost of the election for the candidate, the candidate had to secure at least 5% of the total votes cast, failing which, he would have to forfeit the amount spent on his election. Since all the candidates would have been given equal opportunity in terms of resources, it would be only fair to expect them to convince at least one out of every twenty voters (5%).

c) Accountability: The financial account of the candidates would be maintained and managed by the Election Commission. All the approved candidates would be required to submit their election spending budget, which could go be up to the stipulated ceiling. This would be made public information and the Election Commission would make provision accordingly. Each candidate would have a bank account linked in real time to an electronic box, which would be available in real time for the public to access over the internet and other media. Any objections to the spending could be raised 'as it happens'. Moreover, most of the advertising and campaigning material would be bar coded so that it could be traced back to the account of the candidate.

To strengthen the foundations of the system, strong laws would be needed to swiftly handle cases of financial discrepancies and irregularities. In cases where financial irregularity was reported, a special investigation committee would look into the matter and dispose of the case within a month or less and the guilty would be barred from participating in the political process in the future.

Such a system would make politics a viable option for a new breed of spirited, youthful, energetic and fresh political aspirants with a developmental agenda and innovative bent of mind.

BUILDING UNBREAKABLE PROMISES AND INFALLIBLE DELIVERY

One of the cornerstones of the Western democratic system, especially the American version, is a set of carefully drafted promises in the form of a manifesto. Each political party brings out a well-researched document, with a clearly defined vision encompassing all the aspects of importance including healthcare, education, economy, poverty, food and water, environment and other dimensions of regional importance. This is followed by debates and discussions on the feasibility and merits of the individual manifestoes and rigorous questioning ensures that the people who go to polls are aware of what to expect as a result of their voting preference. In a parliamentary system of democracy such as ours, the role of a manifesto is even more significant as the parliamentarians (or state legislators) are accountable not only for Central planning but also for the development of their own electoral constituency.

Unfortunately, an indifference and lack of commitment in drafting manifestoes is a malaise common across all parties. Most manifestoes in the recent elections lacked a proper vision, little was spoken about the implementation plan and veritably no fruitful debate ever took place upon the merits of the promises being made. Timing of the manifesto further magnifies the apathy. Nearly all the major parties chose to come up with their manifestoes only with less than a month left to the elections, with the last manifesto being brought to public notice almost like a last-minute assignment—sometimes within the final week of polling date!

This situation must transform. If developmental politics has to be the thrust, then the first proposal of a development plan has to emerge in the form of a manifesto which is a direct gauge of the vision of a party and a candidate.

It should be mandatory for every candidate, irrespective of the party affiliation, to draft a manifesto clearly outlining the plan of action and resource acquisition. Candidates can be given guidelines for the purpose. A good starting framework could be the development radar. Each candidate can then get down to implementing his action plan based on the priorities of his constituency and his overall vision.

The responsibility of developing the manifesto, defending the ideas proposed, and accountability for the promises made would solely rest with the candidate. The candidate's manifesto must contain a timeline for delivery with clear demarcations between 'certain deliverables' and 'aspirational items'. Any violations of the 'certain deliverables' on three or more counts would automatically qualify for a recall of the member. Local-level debates between the candidates based on their development manifesto need to be institutionalized and broadcast for the people to make informed judgment.

The same rigorous development manifesto preparation and accountability should be applied to the national and state political parties contesting for the elections. Party leaders, with their individual competencies and experience, should contribute in their expertise areas and then defend their statement against each other and third-party experts. Let us, for example, visualize a formal discussion on the economic health of the nation before the polls. It would be based on the carefully crafted document of the three national parties with the best experts representing the cases of their parties in a nationally followed open debate. This debate could be hosted by one of the Indian Institutes of Management or similar academic institutes, with clearly defined mandate to established yardsticks for the people along the parameters of efficacy, innovation and feasibility of the promises. This would be a chance for people to decide on the potential of the candidates, rather than primarily on their present or past affiliation to a group.

BETTER VOTING REFORMS

As our democracy matures further, we will have to consider more direct and effective rights vested in the vote than merely a choice to 'Select one of the following'. Innovation and political ingenuity would have to be carefully deployed to evolve a mechanism where people can reward and reprimand their representatives in better ways, and exert choices not thought about earlier. The quest is to make the vote more powerful and an effective means of conveying the foremost message of democracy. The underlying expectation here being that when people get a real sense of choices with checks and balances, their participation, and the enthusiasm, will increase. Let us discuss two such revolutionary ideas which hold the key for transforming our democracy to a standard which would be a milestone for the world.

A. Right to Reject

Voting has to have an additional power to go beyond mere selection; it also needs to be empowered with the choice to reject candidates. Many democratic tools have been discussed amongst the experts, some of which also are in implementation in various parts of the world. These include ranking-based voting, negative voting, multiple preferences and the option to choose 'None of the above (or NOTA[2])'. In this section, we will discuss the last of these, NOTA.

The ability to not cast a vote for any of the candidates is already there in Rule 49-O. However, it is insufficient. While, from 2013, the NOTA option is available on the voting machine itself, the intent of the option even now is to prevent votes in the name of people who choose not to cast their ballot by effectively neutralizing their vote. Its purpose to prevent fraud is not the same as people's empowerment to reject all candidates. Secondly, NOTA is of no practical consequence in the results of the elections. Theoretically, even if the majority of ballots were NOTA, it would be of no consequence in the overall results.

One of the foremost reforms which needs serious consideration in a democracy striving to move ahead is to give the people a greater say in terms of voting. In a true democracy, people can be given choices as an opportunity to express themselves unreservedly and in as unrestricted a way as possible. Allowing for a well-structured and consequential option towards 'reject all' is a reform which can create a colossal change in the pace and intensity of democratic reforms emanating from the fundamental tool of democracy—people's vote.

Many nations and states around the world follow the policy of granting the voters an option of rejecting all candidates in different versions and in most of these cases, it exists as a clear and distinct option on the ballot paper itself. Switzerland, Spain, France and Belgium offer a blank vote option. These votes, though not stamped in favour of any candidate, are counted and reported. The US state of Nevada has the option 'None of these candidates', Ukraine has 'Against All', France has 'vote blanc', Spain has 'voto en blanco' and for a long time Russia also had an 'against all' option in voting. Perhaps, the best examples are from the state of Massachusetts in the US and the South American nation of Colombia where the negative vote is of significant consequence. In Colombia, if the blank votes (none of the above) get a majority then the elections are held again. Similarly, in 2006, Massachusetts included 'None of the Above for a New Election' as an option. A majority of votes cast on this option meant a re-poll with the entire set of contesting candidates out of the re-poll.

Article 258 of the Colombian Constitution

Article 258 of the Constitution of Colombia deals with the issue of voting. The article clarifies that when the blank votes constitute a majority of the total valid votes in a ballot to elect members of a public corporation, governor, mayor or in the first round in presidential elections, the elections should be repeated once.

The inclusion of such a right would require the following changes.

  i) Inclusion of the option to reject all candidates as a fundamental right to all the citizens.

 ii) In case the maximum number of votes is received under the 'None of Above' account, fresh elections should be held within one month. In these re-elections, none of the previous candidates or their immediate relatives should be allowed to contest. This would allow a fresh set of political leaders to emerge based on better agenda.

iii) In any event, the number of votes cast under 'None of the above' option must be counted and properly reported.

The addition of a dynamic tool such as this to the voting system will further empower people, which is the basic purpose of a democracy. It would lead to a system which has a mechanism to remove the incompetent and bring in fresh talent. Such a system would be intrinsically powerful enough to bring local-level democratic reforms where the monopoly power of the mighty few could be democratically countered by the right to reject enshrined with the people. It would be an effective check for the contesting parties to field candidates with a clean image and immaculate record. Such a voting system would also help in motivating the people to increase their participation in the process of governance, as no longer would casting your ballot be a decision of selection of one from a wide choice of the undeserving.

B. Right to Recall

The people's right to recall their elected representative has been a much-debated topic in forums for democratic reform. It hinges on the philosophy that just as it is possible to 'fire' an incompetent official, there should be a mechanism to terminate the tenure of an elected representative who is proven to be corrupt or is otherwise irremediably incompetent to discharge the duties as vested upon him or her by the constitution.

The 'right to recall' is an optimal tool for ensuring that specific cases of corruption in the highest elected offices are dealt with surgical precision and weeded out immediately. It would ensure that the 'licence' to be in an elected office irrespective of the quality of service is revoked and real-time accountability is injected into the democratic system.

The right to recall elected representatives is not new. While enacting such a right has been a matter of discussion in almost all the nations, three nations particularly stand out in its implementation—the US, Canada and Venezuela in South America.

**Article 72 of the Venezuelan Constitution
(Right to Recall)**

All [. . .] offices filled by popular vote are subject to revocation. Once one-half of the term of office to which an official has been elected has elapsed, a number of voters representing at least 20% of the registered voters in the affected constituency may petition for the calling of a referendum to revoke that official's mandate.

When a number of voters equal to or greater than the number of those who elected the official vote in favour of the recall, provided that a number of voters equal to or greater than 25% of the total number of registered voters vote in the recall referendum, the official's mandate shall be deemed revoked and immediate action shall be taken to fill the permanent vacancy as provided for by this Constitution and by law.

In the US, the recall device began in the Los Angeles municipality in 1903 and Michigan and Oregon, in 1908, were the first states to adopt recall procedures for state officials. Today, 18 out of the 50 states in the US allow elected officials to be recalled from their positions after a petition by 12–40% of the registered voters. Since its inception the right has been exercised in a number of local elected official recalls like mayors and on two occasions it has also led to the recall of governors: in 1921, North Dakota's Lynn J. Frazier was recalled over a dispute about state-owned industries, and recently, in 2003, California governor Gray Davis was recalled over mismanagement of the state budget to be replaced by Arnold Schwarzenegger. In 1995, British Columbia in Canada also enacted the recall law. If a critical minimum number of petitioners is reached, it would lead to a by-election to decide a possible recall. Venezuela has enabled the option of recall even for its highest office, that of the President, under Article 72 of its constitution.

As a bold step towards greater democratic accountability and empowerment, India too needs to consider adopting and rigorously implementing the option of right to recall. Serious misconduct, criminal activities, corruption and squandering of public money for private consumption and failure to deliver on 'certain' promises in the local development manifesto should be made automatic grounds for initiation of recall proceedings of leaders. These proceedings can be administered by the Election Commission of India. Similarly, in case a threshold number, say 20% of the registered electorate, approach the Election Commission and seek recall, it should also lead to the beginning of the recall proceedings. As with many other countries, the recall election can be held with the people having to indicate their choice for or against the recall. The election can also be accompanied with a set of fresh options for the representation. The recall would be successful if the majority of the people vote in favor of recall and also an alternative candidate secures more votes than the votes for the existing representative in the form of against-recall votes. To establish checks and balances and prevent misuse, recall elections should be allowed only after at least one year of completion of term and only once during the entire term of the representative.

The right to recall can thus be a highly efficient tool for cutting short political tenures which are marked by misguided promises and serious misconduct. It would empower the local watchdog bodies which would be monitoring the representative's performance against the promises made, and in cases of serious discrepancy, may emerge as agencies for initiating people's action for the recall. It would also dissuade the candidates from making undeliverable and impossible promises to the people and work for the constituency throughout their tenure, rather than make a contribution only towards the time when the elections are in near sight. Above all, it would ensure that the people are enabled to curtail corruption, in a real time mode, whenever it occurs.

POLITICAL POLITICS AND DEVELOPMENTAL POLITICS

Politics has two dimensions: 'political' politics and developmental politics. Political politics is essential when elections are to be held and various parties vie for influence. After the election process, however, every nation needs developmental politics that is unique to its needs.

We would like to visualize a situation in which the political parties perform in an environment of developmental politics in any country, competing with each other in putting forth their political vision through their manifesto. It goes like this; let me narrate the sample scenarios:

Suppose **Party A** says, within 10 years, we will lead the nation to economic development and also back our claim with a growth plan for execution. **Party B** says, we will lead the nation to development within 7 years through a clear-cut action plan. **Party C** may unveil a new strategy for national development with different indicators and excel in ideas related to the nation's role in the global arena. It may give a road map to ensure that the nation becomes a permanent member of the United Nations Security Council within a period of five years, for instance, and suggest ideas that lead to the generation of enlightened citizenship.

Normally, the members should spend 30% of their time and effort in dealing with political politics and the remaining 70% should be utilized for promoting development politics. Development politics is the need of the hour, and development politics will require efficient, creative leadership at all levels with spotless integrity.

Not for once can we harbour serious doubts on the efficacy of our political systems and leaders. If an individual is capable of mocking an entire system of complex checks and balances, within a period of four to five years amass wealth of crores of rupees from the people's money, and then again be able to convince the same people to elect him or her again, it would be naïve to cast doubts on the efficiency of the person. The real issue is far more serious than efficiency and far deeper than qualification. It is rooted in a lack of conscience and integrity.

Then, there stands the popular argument of lack of education and prevalence of corruption. While empirically the argument would make sense, yet in the absence of real value-oriented learning, the experiential correlation between the educational qualification and the moral uprightness, even liberally speaking, is meagre. Many of the tainted politicians boast an array of impressive academic degrees. Education alone will not lead to ethical leadership. Knowledge needs to be accompanied by ethics and integrity, only then can creative leadership be nurtured. In the next chapter, we will focus on the evolution of such ethics-based knowledge systems, with teachers who act as role models not just for lessons but life.

'HOW CAN I BE CLEAN?'
THE DILEMMA OF THE YOUNG RECRUIT

In 2010, I accepted an invitation from the Lal Bahadur Shastri National Academy of Administration, Mussoorie[3] to conduct a lecture for the newly recruited Civil Services trainees who would be undergoing their foundation course there. My team, including Srijan and I, landed in Dehradun, the nearest airport, and then proceeded by car up the rugged mountains of the lower Himalayas as we travelled to Mussoorie, a journey of about three hours. We reached the academy a little before sunset. Sitting in that beautiful environment, as we observed the ever so friendly and diligent staff and the young officers, soon to confidently assume important positions, go about their work as the day closed, it signified something most important to me—hope. While there was a lecture ready at hand, seeing them made me decide to try something new for the lecture the next morning. We had a small discussion over dinner about the lecture and the necessary changes were made.

The next morning, 18 October, when I met the beaming men and women who were on the verge of being inducted into the most coveted services in the nation, I chose to talk to them, not about

development and administration, not about the challenges and
opportunities of career, but the answers to a simple question which
I posed to them—'What will I be remembered for?' As I discussed
various missions which they needed to evolve for the nation, I
suggested to them to ask themselves this question. I asked them to
write it on a piece of paper; what they wrote down might well prove
to be something far-reaching and important that they would be
remembered for. It could be something on societal reform, better
governance, an innovative strategy to address the problem of poverty
or environmental degradation, or a way of contributing towards
inclusive growth in a timebound manner. Then I put forth some
innovative ideas for this mission which might start up their thought
process.

1. Will you be remembered for a visionary action for the nation,
   a pioneering reform in society or education?
2. Will you be remembered for creating a vibrant district with
   hundreds of small industries contributing in a meaningful
   way to employment generation?
3. Will you be remembered for becoming a pioneer in
   developing smart waterways in the states and linking of rivers?
4. Will you be remembered for revitalizing or revolutionizing
   the development of integrated primary healthcare centres in
   a public-private-participation model?
5. Will you be remembered for creating a validated system for
   the production of 340 million tonnes of food grains and value
   addition through food processing by 2020?
6. Will you be remembered for bringing energy independence
   for the nation?
7. Will you be remembered for developing one million
   enlightened youth in your region who will participate in the
   accelerated societal transformation of the nation?

The lecture went well, with the participants listening attentively.
The prospect of being a part of history by accomplishing something

extraordinary got them excited. Finally, I asked them to take a ten-point oath. They all loudly repeated the points, full of confidence and exuberance, until I came to the last point of the oath. This was, 'I will work with integrity, and succeed with integrity.' Suddenly, there was a moment of silence in the hall—'Succeed with integrity?' Obviously this was a difficult question I had posed to them, especially in the current context when there is so much discussion of corruption, but then they remembered that they had to work for something unique, and the hall reverberated with the voices of the 200 youth present there: 'I will work with integrity and succeed with integrity.' The spirit with which this was said was a delight to hear.

After the session, some questions were raised by the participants which highlight the opportunities and challenges in governance faced by the nation's bureaucracy. They reflect the dilemmas of a young officer who wishes to do something special for the nation.

I had asked the young officers to find how they can be creative leaders who can pioneer great missions in life. So after the lecture, one young lady officer got up and asked, 'Dr Kalam, the bureaucracy is trained and known for maintaining status quo. How can I then be creative and innovative?' Another young officer said, 'Sir, right now, at the start of our service, we are all upright. We all want to work hard and make a change. But in a decade's time, in spite of our surroundings, how do I still maintain the same values with enthusiasm?' My reply to them was that the young officers entering service have to determine a long-term goal for which they will be remembered. This goal will inspire them at all times during their career and help them overcome all problems. I told them that the young bureaucrats of the nation have to remember that when they take on difficult missions, there will be problems. Problems should not become our masters, we have to defeat the problems and succeed, I told them.

Then came the most interesting question of all. A young officer asked me, 'Dr Kalam, you have asked us to work with integrity and succeed with integrity. But the political system and seniors who are corrupt would definitely put pressure on the young bureaucrats to compromise on their ethical standards. How can we tackle this problem? How do we remain clean in such an environment?' The question was a pertinent one. I responded recalling my own experience where I worked very closely with politicians and administrators in positions like Secretary, Defence Research and Development Organization, Scientific Advisor to the Defence Minister and Principal Scientific Advisor to the Government of India. In all these positions, which were very senior ones, I was in command of large missions with huge capital investments. I recalled that at no point did any leader or administrator, even those who had a not-so-favourable reputation, approach me for favours, ever. Then I told the young officers that they can definitely establish a brand of integrity for themselves which would be like a barrier that kept away all those who wanted to make them compromise their principles. Of course, this might mean facing problems in their career, but the final triumph would be theirs.

It is a time, however, when young officers in various services are all going through a similar dilemma at the start of the service—they want to be unique, they want to the ones who make a difference to the nation and its people—but somehow the system drags their righteous spirit down into corrupted submission. Corruption seemingly becomes more acceptable with time. Why?

One reason for this is the syndrome which affects almost all public services—'seniority surpasses all'. The only way to proceed upwards is to have stayed there, longer the better, and those who are at the top are too far and too secure to be caught in the ropes of accountability. Seniority in government services has become like a caste system which engulfs creativity, talent and honour like a python swallows its prey. 'Stay silent and do what you are told' is not only safe but also lucrative, at least in the short run. There are obvious incentives to walk the dotted line into darkness and disincentives to be different and unique to create a new way of doing things.

A senior IPS officer from Gujarat told an interesting story to Srijan. He talked about a typical scene at an IAS or an IPS reunion party. Whenever there is such a party, comprising officers from different batches, there is an uneasy stiffness for the first fifteen minutes. Everyone goes around, often with their spouse, being self-consciously formal. Amongst the first few questions would be things like 'Which batch?', 'Which year did you join the service?' or in some cases the officers, especially very senior ones, boldly declare their 'year of joining' in their introduction itself. Within the first 15 minutes, the officer's memory may not be able to associate the name with the person, however, with almost perfect certainty he would be able to decipher a condition with respect to each of the others—'Whether he/she is junior to me, senior to me or equal to me.' This hierarchy would determine who you would boss, who would boss you and who you can be friendly and candid with. The 'food chain' has clear power gaps which are pre-determined, fixed and, of course, extremely sacrosanct.

Such rigid vertical hierarchies rarely lead to efficiency or transparency. My own experience of having worked in pioneering and difficult projects with multi-dimensional teams convinces me that flat and creativity-promoting structures of governance are the need of the hour. Let me narrate a personal experience.

This is from the time, more than three decades ago, in 1976, when I was busy with the SLV3 (Space Launch Vehicle) project in VSSC (Vikram Sarabhai Space Centre). For the successful completion of the inertial measuring unit (IMU) project we needed a precision housing unit which could house three accelerometers and three rate-integrating gyros and the connected processing electronics. The weight budget given for the entire IMU was a mere three kilograms. In those days, such a precision housing within this weight budget could be made only by using magnesium alloy. So I was aggressively in search of a foundry which could do this casting, which would be crucial for the SLV-3 flight. I visited a number of industries both in the private and public sector. When I asked them whether they could cast the precision IMU housing, all of them told me that it would take a minimum three months for realizing the casting since they would have to make a metallic mould. But three months was something we could not possibly afford. In a periodic review of the SLV-3 programme by Prof. Satish Dhawan, IMU housing was put on the critical path. Any delays in the IMU would mean significant delays in the entire project realization. Then Prof. Dhawan suggested, 'Kalam! There is a very tall scientist working in DMRL who is a metallurgist. I am sure if you go and tell him your problem, he will be able to help you.' When I reached DMRL, I found the 'tall' scientist was busy with his team in one of the laboratories. This was my first introduction to Dr V.S. Arunachalam. He asked me what my problem was. I told him that I needed a magnesium alloy precision casing for the inertial measuring unit within a weight budget of 3 kg. I also told him, I would like to have one unit of the cast casing for testing within a week. Dr Arunachalam smiled and emphatically said, 'No problem.' Then his smile got wider and he said, 'Kalam! You be with me, I will get it for you within a week.' He called his team members and explained the task. The team studied various options. Dr Arunachalam gave a suggestion that they could cast using a thermocole mould, which was the fastest method to get the casting in time. With this method, I got my casting within a week. While others were thinking of making a regular cast through a metallic die, which is a time-consuming process, Dr Arunachalam gave me an innovative solution immediately to meet my timeframe. This was my first meeting with Dr Arunachalam.

I was not aware of it then, but I would work with him in the DRDO later on for nearly ten years. In 1982 Dr Arunachalam and Dr Raja Ramanna were responsible for my re-entry into DRDO from ISRO. Dr Arunachalam talked to the defence minister, R. Venkataraman (who later became the President of India), who in turn requested Prof. Satish Dhawan to relieve me from ISRO for taking up the directorship of DRDL.

The period 1982–92 was an important decade for the DRDO. During this period three major programmes were sanctioned due to the leadership of Dr Arunachalam. One was the Integrated Guided Missile Development Programme (IGMDP), the second was a light combat aircraft and the third was the Advanced Technology Vehicle (ATV) programme. This is the first time the DRDO budget was increased from 2% of the defence budget to 4%. A Board of Management structure was created for IGMDP, a society structure was created for LCA and a hybrid structure was created for the ATV. The DRDO graduated in this period from being an import substitution establishment to a full-fledged system design and development organization. The strength of scientists in the DRDO also grew to six thousand. Dr V.S. Arunachalam was responsible for introducing these innovations in the DRDO.

I especially recall an incident which happened when we were preparing for the Agni launch in 1989. We were at the Chandipur range in Orissa. A day before D-day we had the launch authorization board meeting, which, as one would expect, was an occasion for many debates and discussions. All of us were determined to successfully complete the project, which would propel India many steps up the ladder of missile technology. Our tireless planning and evaluation went on right up to 2 a.m. in the morning of the launch day. After the meeting Dr Arunachalam and I were returning to the guest house from the block house where we had conducted the meeting. It was a relatively long drive, through meandering roads. On the way, I seem to have slept in the car. None of the bumps and turns of the path woke me up. When we reached the guest house, the car stopped. Dr Arunachalam gently tapped me and I woke up. I found my head had been on his shoulder all along. I felt very embarrassed; after all he was my boss. All along the journey he didn't want to disturb me by moving my head. Such was the man. I wonder, in today's bureaucracy, will any boss be so tolerant. Of course, Dr Arunachalam was not a boss, he was always a friend. Hierarchies were superseded by friendship. This was the culture, hierarchies were not so important to us.

THE CASE OF ABSOLUTE POWER ABSOLUTELY CORRUPTS

Power gap—the difference between those with privilege and those without—has been fundamental to our society. From ancient times, power gaps were systematically introduced into society first via a rigid mechanism of caste, then through favouritism to courtiers and elites in the medieval period, both of which created a class of privileged people who were by status or the power of brute force beyond being called to account. The British nurtured the mechanism by creating a class of English-speaking administrators who helped them run the show, without being answerable to the common man. Unfortunately, our inheritance of the same civil service structure has meant that the virus of power gap has found its way into our current system of administration as well. But that is only one side of it. Over time, a complex arrangement of money and manipulation has widened the power gap. At their worst, the consequences of such a distortion of power structures become evident when an IIM graduate like S. Manjunathan or a grassroot RTI activist like Satish Shetty are casualties of challenging the structure and its corrupt manifestations.

The problem with a society with such disparity is that it creates individuals, entities and institutions which are beyond question and scrutiny. The immunity from questioning transcends into lack of transparency which promotes corruption. Facts bear this out. One of the prominent measures of Power Gap in a society is called Hofstede's Power Distance Index, which objectively measures the extent to which the less powerful members of organizations and institutions accept and expect that power is distributed unequally. Thus it measures inequality from bottom up rather than the other way round on the basis that in a society inequality is endorsed by the follower more than the leader. For establishing the link between corruption in a nation and the Power Gap in its society we will map its Corruption Perception Index (CPI) ranking versus Hofstede's Power Distance Index (PDI). A higher score on CPI indicates less

corruption and a higher score on PDI indicates a higher degree of
power gap in society.

Corruption ranking (least corrupt to most corrupt)	Nation	CPI Score (10 = least corrupt, 0 = most corrupt)	Hofstede's Power Distance Index (PDI) Score
1	Denmark	9.30	18
1	New Zealand	9.30	22
1	Singapore	9.30	74
4	Finland	9.20	33
4	Sweden	9.20	31
7	Netherlands	8.80	38
8	Australia	8.70	36
8	Switzerland	8.70	34
10	Norway	8.60	31
13	Hong Kong	8.40	68
15	Austria	7.90	11
15	Germany	7.90	35
20	United Kingdom	7.60	35
21	Chile	7.20	63
22	Belgium	7.10	65
22	United States	7.10	40
24	Uruguay	6.90	61
25	France	6.80	68
30	Israel	6.10	13
30	Spain	6.10	57
50	Saudi Arabia	4.70	80
53	Czech Republic	4.60	57
54	Kuwait	4.50	80
54	South Africa	4.50	49

Corruption ranking (least corrupt to most corrupt)	Nation	CPI Score (10 = least corrupt, 0 = most corrupt)	Hofstede's Power Distance Index (PDI) Score
78	China	3.50	80
84	India	3.80	77
98	Egypt	3.10	80
98	Mexico	3.10	81
110	Indonesia	2.80	78
134	Nigeria	2.40	77
134	Philippines	2.40	94

TABLE 1: Corruption ranking of different countries

There is a strong link between the Power Distance and the level of corruption in the system. This is so as in most cases, once the most corrupt go up to assume power, it gets very easy for them to create an iron fence around themselves that is hard to breach. Power Distance also closes the option of scrutiny of every action for integrity and transparency and breeds a culture of sycophancy which promotes absolute corruption.

THE CORRUPTION POTENTIAL

Based on the above examples and experiences, let us now try to derive what are the fundamental factors which determine the vulnerability of a governance system to the menace of corruption. There are three keys attributes of a system.

- Incentive to do corruption, which determines how easy or difficult it is for the corrupt to survive and thrive
- Incentive to work efficiently with good governance
- Support system for those who are willing to fight against corruption internally.

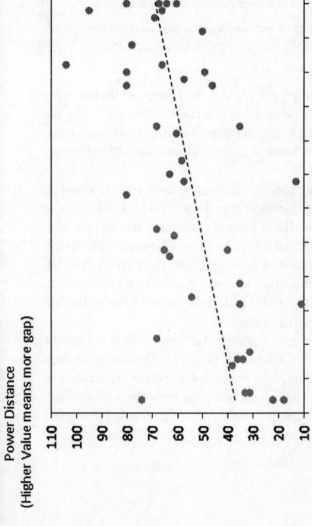

Power Distance
(Higher Value means more gap)

10-CPI
(Higher value means less corruption)

FIGURE 2: Relationship between power gap and corruption perception

With these points in mind, we can identify the factors which
determine the corruption potential in an organization or an
institution.

> **Potential for Corruption in Governance**
>
> **= Monopoly Power with Subjective Discretion**
>
> **x Perceived Amnesty from Prosecution**
>
> **x Uncertainty of Tenure with lack of accountability**

Monopoly Power

The current system of governance, including the bureaucracy
and the judiciary, has descended to what used to exist during the
British Raj. The Indian Civil Service of the 'Raj era' has undergone
little change besides being renamed as the Indian Administrative
Service.

A district collector today is in charge of about five to six million
people, which would correspond to a small country of Europe in
terms of population. He is the one who takes the call on what
benefits who will get and when, he is the centrepiece that moves
(or stops) the movement of essential goods and services, he allots
funds, checks the execution of projects and welfare schemes. In
most places, especially in the hinterland and the villages, the IAS
or IPS officer is treated as a king.

There is another aspect as well. The civil services are run by
generalists, and in the absence of people's awareness about their
rights, even where things go wrong, few questions are asked. The
bureaucracy is first empowered and then protected with the high
walls of protection against prosecution—that is how monopolies
are created and nurtured.

Accountability at the Highest Levels

Marcus Einfeld was a Federal Court Judge (similar to India's Supreme Court) for over fifteen years, a lawyer in the UK and Australia for over two decades and the founder of the Australian Human Rights Commission. In 2006, while driving in the city of Sydney, Marcus was caught by a speed camera, overspeeding by 10 kilometres per hour, it was alleged. Under the Australian system, the fine for the offence would have been about $75 and loss of points on the driver's licence, which was a minor punishment. However, Marcus claimed that it was not he who was driving. On oath, he said that he had lent the car to US academic Teresa Brennan and blamed her for the mistake. The story would have been believed, but a newspaper journalist, through mere internet search, discovered that Brennan had passed away in 2003, some three years earlier.

This was immediately taken as a breach of the highest order and Marcus, a judge himself, was tried for a deliberate act to mislead justice and found guilty. He was stripped of his Queen's Counsel title and sentenced to three years of imprisonment, it is reported.

Perceived Amnesty from Prosecution

While there are laws laid down against corruption and there are agencies entrusted with enforcing them, the ground reality about the corrupt and the corrupted is, too few are ever brought to justice and it simply takes too long for justice to have any significant impact. Sometimes, these delays are system induced, due to pendency in court, and sometimes they are people induced, where there are deliberate lapses in the investigation or execution to protect the corrupt.

A senior IPS officer from Uttar Pradesh, who also served in the state vigilance department, narrated a story that highlights the problem. He said in the late 1970s there was an enquiry conducted by the vigilance department against a government engineer for corruption. The enquiry was swift as the case was backed with evidence and soon the concerned department was sent a recommendation to suspend the engineer. Then nothing happened for a few months. The vigilance department followed up with another reminder, only to be met with silence and inaction. The process went on for months, then years and eventually decades. The eerie silence was finally broken, in 1992, after two full decades had passed since the recommendation for action against the engineer, in a short reply from the department which said: 'The concerned officer has retired last month, hence this recommendation for suspension cannot be executed. Thank you.'

Justice comes with an expiry date—without a time limit to deliver, it fades into irrelevance. Absence of swift and decisive action in cases of corruption has a doubly negative impact. First, with time, the corrupt only become stronger in stature with the power of acquired money, influence and sheer audacity created by not getting caught. Second, the act of seeing the corrupt getting the benefits of delays in justice being delivered is demoralizing for others who value integrity and soon the fence-sitters are likely to follow the path of corruption. Honesty, rather than corruption, seems to come at a price. Delays in justice create the path from individual corruption to institutional corruption.

Delivery of justice in the case of corruption needs a very special consideration, as in most cases the involved are in a position to influence the process of investigation and justice. It is a common observation that cases of corruption are generally what is termed at the classical 80:20 ratio. What it means is that 80% of the cases are open and shut, with a bagful of evidence and little scope for doubt, while 20% are complicated, circumspect and need careful scrutiny. The problem is that as a system we treat them in the same basket and hence the speed of justice and action flows at the slowest possible speed. This issue of the '80%' flowing at the speed of '20%' needs to be resolved. How?

a) We need to establish a Fundamental Code for Conduct for Public Service, which is a set of basic criteria which if not fulfilled by any public servant would amount to breach of integrity and hence corruption. The code should have designated punishments for corruption, defined objectively, delivered in a timebound manner, and in a language the common man can understand so that there is little scope for subjective discretion. Everyone, the public servicemen and the end users of public services, should be able to understand what act of corruption would attract which punishment. These would be the most basic and clear cases, often with clear evidence, the 80% bulk would have to be dealt with by swift action within a month of the breach. A traffic policeman caught red-handed accepting bribes on the roadside, a minister on video accepting payment for a favourable deal in a contract or an army colonel taped dealing with purported arms dealers are open and shut cases that need not go through the chain of a 3-tier judicial system. The fear of clear and quick action will certainly curb corruption even if it will not eradicate it.

b) India, with its vast academic potential and premier institutions of technology and management like the IITs and IIMs needs to be engaged in mapping the integrity, competency and efficiency of the public services in the respective states, thereby creating an Inter Departmental Integrity Index.

We have about 15 IITs and 12 IIMs spread across the nation—it would be of great help if these institutions can be used as independent analysts to rate and rank each of the departments with regard to integrity and competence. The information obtained would serve as a benchmark to isolate corrupt practices and also to highlight the cases of success. It will also help in taking action against those divisions or departments which are shown to have rampant corruption.

TOWARDS MISSION MODE GOVERNANCE: CREATING ROBUST PUBLIC SERVICE STRUCTURES

In the long run, there have to be far more fundamental systemic alterations in the system of public services and governance. In the

British Raj, there was only one need to fulfilled—English-speaking Indian youth who maintained the status quo. Of course this meant to maintain law and order, collect revenues, see to the comfort of the British officers and maintain the given public utilities. Free India cannot run on an archaic system designed to force a nation to be permanently on crutches. We have already observed how the powers and incentives are concentrated in a few hands, which leads to corruption. The system has all the incentives for orthodoxy and risks are heavily against those who choose to be creative.

Let us analyse three highly successful organizations. The first is the Delhi Metro Rail Corporation, a project which has managed the timely construction, operation and maintenance of a vast network of lines through the city and towns nearby. Furthermore, not at a single moment was it accused of fund mismanagement—a rare feat in a construction project. A second example is the Indian Space Research Organization (ISRO), which has taken India into the elite club of space-faring nations using the minimum possible resources. The third example is a project from the Defence Research and Development Organization (DRDO). This is the BrahMos project, which is a supersonic cruise missile development and production initiative drawing upon the core competencies of multiple nations which is now doing remarkable business for the nation. What is common to all these organization? It is the fact that they are all mission-mode oriented and that they have leaders who are not only inspirational in their work culture but also are subject experts in their respective domains. The visionary Prof. Vikram Sarabhai and all the ISRO chiefs who followed him were people who knew more about space and space technologies than anyone else in the nation. E. Sreedharan, who headed the Delhi Metro Rail Corporation, has done outstanding work in civil engineering and had an excellent track record in the railways. Dr A. Sivathanu Pillai, who is the CEO and MD of BrahMos, is an expert on launch vehicles and missile technologies. The system so developed is precisely on target delivering enormous kinetic energy due to its supersonic speed. In the successful design, development, production and marketing of BrahMos, an innovative way of technology co-operation has emerged between India and Russia that has generated nearly $7 billion worth of business with an investment of $150 million from each partner.

The Case of Specialist Leadership at Delhi Metro Rail Corporation

The Delhi Metro Rail Corporation is a pioneering project which has now been successfully executed in the capital Delhi and the nearby cities of Gurgaon and Noida. The project has given to the nation the potential of executing a fast transportation system using high technology with reliability through a timebound mission-mode operation. Delhi, with a population of over 14 million, has the distinction of having a world-class metro rail with frontline technologies. Work on the metro rail commenced on October 1998 and the first phase with three lines covering 66 km was completed by December 2005. The second phase with 121 km of line length was completed in 2010. The Delhi Metro was a complicated project owing to the fact that it involved complex construction work in densely populated and built-up areas within a tight schedule, and had to do this without deviating from high standards of reliability, without losing out on cost effectiveness.

The project has been a marvellous success. Often the implementation has been completed well before deadline and within budget. What was the single most important attribute for this success?

It is the fact that it is led by a team of specialists in construction and operation of railways. Its Managing Director, Elattuvalapil Sreedharan, who is now a household name nationally, is one of the best civil engineers India has produced in modern times. He has a reputation of managing difficult civil construction work with utmost transparency. Remarkably, he took on this challenging and difficult assignment post retirement.

> With an expert team at the helm of affairs, it is far easier to manage a project with transparency as each member of the top management understands the ground realities of the work involved. The DMRC is a prime example of how specialist leadership can make a difference in creating a clean, efficient organization.

There is something fundamentally wrong when one sees someone who is well learned in Political Science and History step into the role of directing the nation's environment policy or is asked to handle the financial secretariat. Often times, it appears a case of mismatching of skills with roles.

In a scenario where we aspire to be a developed nation by 2020, the methods of yesterday will fail dismally to have the desired effects.

For long, perhaps since the inception of the civil services, we have overly relied on a model which we could call the 'Generalist Centric Approach'. With the rapid progress in technology and changing needs of the nation the 'generalists' at the centre now surround themselves with a crowd of specialists who can assist in decision making.

However, non-specialists as final decision makers are not sufficiently motivated as they are not well equipped to foresee the future impact of key decisions. They can be easily misled by a stakeholder into making wrong plans and implement them in an erratic manner. Often the allegiance between the advisor and the specialist is based on how the personal equations balance out rather than the quality of the inputs given. It is reminiscent of a 16th century monarch, who knew little about the kingdom except what he was told by his trusted councillors. They can at best be expected to do what seems safest to them—maintain the status quo.

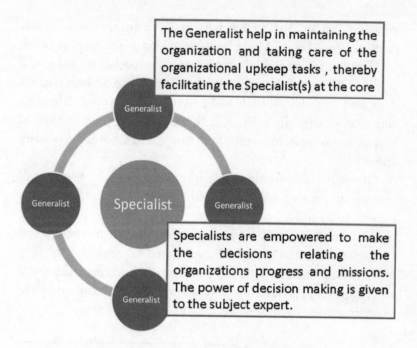

The Generalist help in maintaining the organization and taking care of the organizational upkeep tasks , thereby facilitating the Specialist(s) at the core

Specialists are empowered to make the decisions relating the organizations progress and missions. The power of decision making is given to the subject expert.

FIGURE 3: Generalist-centric Approach

Having 'generalists' without consideration for their specific expertise is good for roles which need experience and guidelines—especially those requiring upkeep of law and order and functions like justice and revenue. However, when it comes to making and executing policy for the billion, there is a stark need for specialist talent—it requires the best in the field that can unravel intricacies with integrity. Furthermore, with India becoming a knowledge powerhouse, by not getting specialists in key decision-making roles we are missing out on the knowledge dividend which the nation can harness for clean development.

There is a need for a substantial overhaul in the bureaucratic system to promote creative and specialist leadership. The new approach would require a shift in the structure of recruitment where the higher level bureaucratic positions need not come through seniority alone but also through exemplary work in the concerned sector. This approach we shall call the Specialist Centric Approach for Mission Mode Implementation as shown in figure 4.

Here the senior administrators would be specialists who would act like CEOs and the department will work like an organization dedicated to public service and progress. They would define, in consultation with the relevant authorities, a long-term vision and mid-term (two-year) missions which would lead towards the primary vision.

Of course, this would mean institutionalizing a new way of bureaucratic entry—lateral hires, which would mean that domain experts from a variety of backgrounds, academia, consultants, industry leaders, social leaders, professionals, engineers, doctors and scientists could directly be appointed to head the mission-mode-centric organizations and departments. Such an institutional mechanism for lateral entry into administration already exists in many countries, including the US, Australia and France.

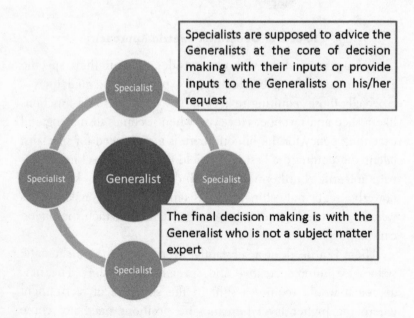

FIGURE 4: The Specialist-Centric Approach for Mission Mode Implementation

There are already some successful examples of such lateral entry into administration, a notable one being Sam Pitroda who was brought in by the then prime minister to overhaul telecom in the country and, more recently, Nandan Nilekani, who was appointed chairman of the Unique Identification Authority of India. Even former Prime Minister Manmohan Singh as finance minister in the 1990s and specialists in their respective fields like I.G. Patel and Sam Pitroda were lateral hires into governance.

It will not be enough to have specialists. It will be important to provide them the freedom and opportunity to do their task efficiently and well. Whenever I have come across an honest officer, who has stood up to the machinations of corrupt bosses, one tool of 'punishment' employed against them has been that of frequent transfers, I have found.

	General-centric	Specialist-centric
Model	Administration	Leadership and Management
Planning	Historic	Innovation
Incentive	Low risk and low return	Better delivery and profits
Outcome	Status quo at best	Rapid growth
Transparency	Less as the leader is faintly acquainted with the systems	Higher as the leader is the expert in the domain
Needs	Long tenure service with timebound promotion	Lateral entry and exit with performance-based promotion

TABLE 2: Summary of comparison between the two approaches

Civil services are one of the most competitive in the world and some of the country's best talent finds its place there. So, besides the structural flaws, what stops them from delivering the optimal results with ethics and transparency? Let us now discuss another issue which needs attention—the uncertainty of tenure.

Short tenures seem to be the norm in many states. This needs serious thought as it has a multi-pronged effect. First, it discourages the officers from evolving and implementing any long-term plan in their department. Second, much of their focus is either in protecting their own posting or dislodging someone else from his or her position—internal politicking is encouraged at the obvious cost of efficiency. Thirdly, transfer-posting is one of the biggest money-minting businesses in top circles of the administration, which needs to be curbed immediately. Fourthly, frequent transfers do not help in building and nurturing competencies in the officers and their positions. Lastly, often the transfers are a function of the political allegiance. Hence having a fragile system of transfers forces bureaucrats to form alliances and proximities with the political masters. These facts are further highlighted as shown in the box.

Lateral Hiring in Bureaucracy

This is a story which dates back to when the nation was gaining independence.

There was a barrister from Chennai who travelled to England to get an additional degree in Economics from the prestigious London School of Economics. He then took up a government job and became a professor in Economics. Somewhere in the middle of his career he moved to politics and entered the legislative council. He then switched back to government service and this time became the director general of statistics. After a few years he again changed jobs, this time joining the private sector as Vice Chairman in Tata Steel and then Tata Motors. Next he became an academic as President of the Indian Institute of Science. Once India became independent, he came back into politics becoming the railways and finance minister of the nation. This is the story of John Mathai. More importantly, it is a story of how talent flowed freely between the private, academic, political and civil services sectors, with each changeover bringing in fresh experience and ideas

---

into the system. This is the institutional strategy we need to introduce in our bureaucracy and civil services through a structured format for lateral entry and exit.

Lateral hiring means that above entry-level bureaucrats can be directly hired, choosing from a range of experts from NGOs, industry, agriculture, technology and academics. These can be permanent or limited term, depending on the need.

Lateral entry exists in many of the developed countries. Australia, for instance, has introduced a system where for senior positions in the civil services, direct advertisements are placed and people from the private sector are interviewed and given the job.

Lateral entry has multiple benefits. First and foremost of these is that it promotes the creation of a specialist-centric organization which by its nature is more efficient and resistant to corruption.

Second, it promotes exchange of ideas. The best way to bring in out-of-the-box thinking into public administration is to introduce people from outside into the system.

Third, with a resurgent nation the very requirement of civil services is moving from mere administration to innovative management and leadership, aspects which lateral hiring would help facilitate.

Just as previously we had suggested fixed tenures for elected governments, here also we strongly recommend establishing a fixed tenure for government positions. For this an amendment would be necessary in the service rules. Depending on position and the responsibilities, fixed tenures can be set ranging from two years to five years.

But more needs to be done.

Clear accountability also needs to be maintained with granting of fixed tenure. Before the role is given to a particular official, a clear set of service deliverables should be established with mutual consent and circulated to the people and other civic bodies. These deliverables should be objective, timebound, realistic and impactful. Unless the official meets these criteria, the guarantee of fixed tenure would stand automatically revoked.

Travelling Bureaucrats (CL)

Short Stays

Average Tenure of an IAS Officer : about 16 months

44% of District Officers are transferred within the first year

Political Correlations

A new chief minister whose party replaces the one previously ruling is twice as likely to transfer bureaucrats than a chief minister who is re-elected.

The average rate of a bureaucrat's transfer increases significantly by 10% over the normal rate when there is a new chief minister. Most of the transfers take place within the first four months of the new chief minister taking office.

CREATING A CULTURE OF PRIDE IN GOVERNANCE

Corruption is not just an economic termite, it is a moral menace which like a worm gnaws away at a citizen's peace of mind. Knowing which strings to pull to enforce your rights becomes important. And then having the capacity to manage the painful intervening period between right violated and right granted is the key. The worst hit are those who are not 'plugged' into the right sources of power.

For example, it is estimated that the Below Poverty Line population of the nation paid a consolidated yearly bribe of Rs 900 crore for basic human needs, like items under public distribution, healthcare and education services, subsidies on agricultural products, rightfully earned wages and for grants and loans for enterprise creation, all of which were theirs as a matter of right. Some time back there were newspaper reports of Rs 2,000 being charged to register a person as being Below Poverty Line, which is roughly about five times the maximum that a Below Poverty Line individual would be making every month! Poor governance can establish such endless downward spirals for the deprived, widen gaps between the rich and the poor which can culminate in violence, left extremism being just one example of it. If citizens are to be bonded in a common thread of national identity, we need to first generate national pride based on good governance and efficient performance.

GEORG1A

The world's number one reformer
2005-2010

The number one easiest place to do business in Eastern and Central Europe and the entire post-Soviet region.

We've done it by undergoing huge change both politically and economically and we plan to grow even more quickly in the future.

To find out how to become part of Georgia's big success story please visit georgia.gov.ge

grow with

FIGURE 5: Georgia advertisement for reforms

Some days back we were both travelling to the US and the air hostess brought us a popular magazine on international politics and economics. As we turned the cover, we found an interesting advertisement on the inside, given in the accompanying figure. It was not a luxury product or service being offered, but an advertisement by a small country in Eastern Europe, Georgia, which was formerly a part of the USSR. It was ravaged by war, both internal and external, and its economy was in shambles. But now the country was trying to recover and show to the world that it had executed colossal reforms and was using this proposition to attract business and investment through the international magazine. There is a lesson to be learnt from this country, one much smaller in size and population, which had the misfortune to get caught up in conflicts that crippled its economy, a nation which was in transition from Communism to the liberal economy of its newfound neighbours in Europe. This is the lesson of shared national pride and image which good governance and a reformist agenda can bring about. This will be our biggest competitive advantage in a world and a century which is predicted to be increasingly impacted by India.

8

WATER EQUATIONS AND THE RIGHT TO WATER FOR ALL

In 2014, we both travelled to Edinburgh, where we visited the library of the University of Edinburgh. The library is a beautiful and historic monument—filled with handwritten books by famous scientists and thinkers—including the original copy of *On the Origin of Species* by Charles Darwin. The vast building is spread across multiple stories and has huge reading spaces used by students and professors alike.

We decided to sit in this space of learning—frequented by the likes of Alexander Graham Bell, Charles Darwin, Thomas Bayes, Sir Walter Scott, Sir Arthur Conan Doyle and many others. In this extraordinary library, our discussions meandered into the major international issues affecting humankind. Soon some of the students around us joined in and, without any plan, we had created a dynamic classroom in the library. Then, one student said, the greatest challenge of our times is drinking water! Another student supported the notion and soon most of them agreed—we must solve the challenge of providing everyone clean water. From then on, our discussion solely focused on the role of clean water in the international arena.

Four years before this spontaneous discussion, in 2010, while both of us were at the University of Kentucky in the US, we interacted and worked with a group of about fifty students from various disciplines who were working on innovations to change the world. Interestingly, twenty of these were working on innovations to provide clean drinking water. Four years later, across the Atlantic, and despite being in a developed world where tapwater was safe enough to drink, the mind of the youth was still identifying drinking water as the biggest international challenge.

Indeed the challenge is mighty. Across the world, 783 million people have no access to clean and safe water.[1] As much as 80% of global diseases are linked to poor water conditions and these patients fill up half of the total hospital beds worldwide. Children are the worst victims of unclean drinking water. Nearly one out of every five deaths under the age of 5 worldwide is due to a water-related disease.[2] As much as 443 million schooldays are lost each year due to water-related diseases. What is most remarkable, however, is that, according to the World Health Organization, for every $1 invested in water and sanitation, there is an economic return of between $3 and $34.[3]

India is rapidly becoming a focal point of the issues arising from poor availability of drinking water. Approximately 334 million Indians still lack access to safe drinking water.[4] Diarrhoea alone, exclusively circulated by poor drinking water, causes more than 1,600 deaths daily—more than one child dying every minute due to consumption of pathogen-loaded drinking water. The World Bank estimates that 21% of communicable diseases in India are related to unsafe water.[5] Estimates are that the cost of problems related to poor drinking water is about $4.2 billion or about Rs 26,000 crore annually.[6] The worst side of the problem is that this cost is almost exclusively borne by the economically deprived, especially the rural population.

Water is a fundamental human right. Nature gives us clean water, whether it be in the rivers or as rain. It is the rampant pollution into the rivers, both organic and inorganic, which makes this gift of nature unfit for human consumption. To understand this better, let us analyse the case of the Yamuna—which is the lifeline of Delhi—the city home to both of us. Delhi generated about 1,900,000,000 litres (1.9 billion) of sewage per day. Out of this, 54% is treated by the responsible bodies. Hence, about 874,000 million litres of untreated sewage enters the Yamuna—every day! The Yamuna travels only about 22 km in Delhi—2% of its total length. But this short journey proves fatal for the river—as nearly 70% of the total pollution load into the Yamuna comes from these 22 km only. Yamuna, the lifeline of Delhi, now releases ammonia gas into the air that causes difficulty in breathing and permanent damage to the lungs. It also releases hydrogen sulphide which smells like rotten eggs, and causes bronchitis, asthma and headache. The excessive pollution of the Yamuna has resulted in the obliteration of all life in the river.

Biochemical Oxygen Demand (BOD)

It measures the rate of oxygen used by biological organisms in the water body to decompose the organic matter. This organic matter is often brought by polluted sewerage or industrial effluents.

High BOD indicates that the level of dissolved oxygen is falling. Since aquatic species like fish need oxygen, high BOD indicates that a river's marine life and biodiversity are in danger. It is caused by the presence of high levels of organic pollutants and nitrates in the water body.

To support aquatic life, water should have 4.0 mg/l dissolved oxygen. Its range in the Yamuna between Delhi and Agra is 0.0 mg/l and 3.7 mg/l. Furthermore, water pollution is estimated by measuring its BOD levels and the permissible range is 3 mg/l or less. Whereas the most polluted stretch of the Yamuna has 14–28 mg/l BOD concentration. The lifeline of Delhi is on the verge of becoming a river of death. The story of the Yamuna is not unique— it is repeated across any river system in the nation. The worst befalls whenever the river enters a major city.

At the other end of the spectrum is the fact that the same rivers are supplying drinking water to city dwellers. The water treatment plants are underequipped, often outdated in technology. Coupled with a piping network which is mediocre at best, they are supplying substandard water which is time and again assessed as not 'even fit for bathing'. Often this supply is erratic in time. One of the authors, who lived in the East of Kailash area in south Delhi, had to regularly get up at 4 a.m. to fill the tanks—as the water in the pipes would come only from 4 to 5 a.m. every day. Even a delay of fifteen minutes would send the entire colony into an early morning panic. Poor access to water is not only a cause of poor health but also an issue of major discomfort to many Indians.

In other cases, when drinking water comes from boreholes, the excessive extraction coupled with unplanned recharge has led to sharp drop in water levels. Delhi is filled with over 500,000 illegal boreholes which suck up the groundwater.[7] In the city of Ahmedabad, on average water was available at 63 metres depth in 1997. By 2011, the depth had crossed 100 metres.[8] The trouble is, when one digs so deep for water, the salt content in the water goes up and makes it unfit for consumption. Of course, it also pushes up the cost of extraction of the water.

All these are well-reported stories, which keep appearing at regular intervals. No wonder, the youth from Kentucky and Edinburgh were well aware of these challenges when they identified drinking water as a global crisis which needs to be solved.

★

Clearly, we need a comprehensive roadmap to ensure clean drinking water for both urban and rural India. We are a nation which guarantees free education with free cooked lunch for its children and free or highly subsidized food for about 70% of the population under the Mid-day Meal Scheme, Right to Education and Right to Food. Can we now give a serious thrust towards the Right to Clean Drinking Water? Would 4 litres of daily supply of treated water be a possible dream for a nation which sees a death every minute?

What could be the resources needed, technologies deployed and institutions involved for such a system?

As early as in 1984 (in Bandhua Mukti Morcha vs. Union of India case), the Supreme Court developed the concept of right to 'healthy environment' as part of the 'right to life' under Article 21. The Supreme Court has stated that the right to access clean drinking water is fundamental to life and there is a duty on the State under Article 21 to provide it to its citizens. Legality aside, for a nation which loses more children to unsafe water than any other cause, the right to clean water is not only a part of the right to life but also imperative to secure its future.

Can we simply supply 100% drinkable water in our piped network? In many nations, this is true but we believe it might be slightly difficult, at least on a universal scale, in India for two reasons. First, the piped coverage in the nation is limited—more than two-thirds of the rural drinking water supply comes from tube-wells, hand-pumps and wells.[9] Secondly, even in urban areas, where nearby three-quarters of the population relies on taps and piped network, there will be a problem of ensuring optimal consumption. Treated water is expensive, and its wastage needs to be avoided—which is difficult to do under the current piping system. Hence, while we are all for high-quality water in the piped system, we also realize it needs to be made 'smart' in order to ensure that the 4 litre per individual per day requirement is met and yet any excessive drawing reduced.

More importantly, what about the rural areas where the sparse and scattered population is not an ideal candidate for piped system? And then, there is the issue in urban zones of many slums areas which are unconnected with piped system.

We need a technological breakthrough for this to happen. One such solution is that of Water ATMs. Each Water ATM can be considered as a water-storage tank, which either has an in-built high-quality water purification system or needs to be recharged with filtered water regularly.

The ATM is linked to a centralized water cloud—which fixes an entitlement of litres of water per individual per day. This cloud is mapped against the Universal Citizen Identification (UID) database and also with a mobile phone registration database. It is also linked with bank accounts—to ensure deductions for overdrawing beyond the quota.

All water ATMs can be managed by local entrepreneurs, kirana stores (small-scale retail outlets), community organizations or self-help groups. This model should work as a revenue generator for the operator—and strict norms for quality control and availability should be established and made a necessary criterion for payment.

All citizens need to be given an entitlement of 4 litres of clean water for drinking every day. This entitlement can also be based on the family requirement to enable a single person to collect water for the whole family. Citizens need to arrive at their nearest Water ATM, located in schools, colleges, institutions and public places. They need to authenticate themselves using their fingerprint (biometric) to link to UID database or through mobile-based One-time Password (OTP) to link to the mobile phone number authentication. The person can choose to draw for an individual or family, or overdraw (beyond the free zone of 4 litres per person) and thereby pay directly for the excess from his linked bank account or a prepaid card based on the mobile phone, as mobile money.

Once the person enters the biometric data or OTP for water disbursement, the Water ATM will check for verification with the necessary database. Upon verification from the National Water Cloud, the water will be released for the person or his family as the case maybe. A schematic diagram of this is shown in figure 1.

What would be the cost of such a system? There are four key components to this system—the cost of water purification, cost of the ATM, transportation and management cost and enterprise profit margin. The cost of purification, even at the best possible methodology, is a mere Rs 0.07 per litre.

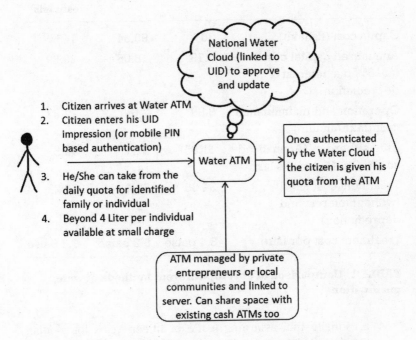

FIGURE 1: Schematic diagram of working of Water ATM

Particulars	Primary treatment system	Primary+ ultra filtration system	Primary+ ultra-filtration system+ reverse osmosis
Capita cost (Rs lakh)	30	90.64	145
Annualized capital cost (@15% p.a. interest & depreciation	5.79	18.06	29.69
Operation and maintenance cost (lakh/annum)	5.88	7.04	12.63
Annual burden (Annualized cost + O & M cost) Rs lakh	11.85	27.1	42.5
Treatment cost Rs/kl (without interest and depreciation)	34.08	52.4	73.22
Treatment cost per Litre	3.4 paise	5.2 paise	7.3 paise

TABLE 1: Comparison of cost for different methods of water purification[10]

We estimate that assuming a life of fifteen years for a solar-powered Water ATM, the annual cost would be about Rs 40,000 per year per Water ATM. Assuming a Rs 0.05 per litre cost of transportation and Rs 0.07 cost of purification, an enterprise-driven model for rollout of Water ATM-based implementation for Right to Water is shown in the table.

Water Right per person per day in litres	4
Number of Water ATMs needed (one per village and additional 25% for urban coverage)	750,000
Population covered (excluding economically secured group of top one-third)	700,000,000
Litres of water per day to be distributed	2,800,000,000

Litres per Water ATM per day to be generated	3,733
Litres per Water ATM to be generated per year	1,362,667
Annualized cost of creating a solar-powered ATM	40,000
Purification cost per litre of water	0.07
Transportation cost per litre of water	0.05
Total purification cost per Water ATM per year	95,387
Total transportation cost per Water ATM per year	68,133
Profit Margin for entrepreneur	12.5%
Net cost per Water ATM per year	228,960
Total cost of Right to Water per year	Rs 17,172 crore
	$2.65 billion

TABLE 2: Cost analysis for the right to water implementation

Under this optimal scenario, covering over two-thirds of the entire population—and making clean drinking water available within 2 km reach for every household, thereby establishing 750,000 Water ATMs—the annual cost would be about Rs 17,000 crore.

Does this make sense? We believe the answer to this question is simple. We had stated earlier that poor drinking water-related problems cost about US$4.2 billion or about Rs 26,000 crore annually. Hence, every rupee spent in Right to Water will earn Rs 1.50 from the first year itself. In the process it will create about 750,000 direct entrepreneurs, and hence about 1.5 to 2.5 million jobs spread across the villages of the nation. It would save the one million people, mostly children, who perish every year to diarrhoea. It would eliminate diseases such as typhoid which affects 1.4 million Indians every year, or significantly solve such age-old problems as those of cholera, E. coli and hepatitis A. Such an intervention will increase the productivity of the workforce, especially at the base of the pyramid, improve attendance in schools and ensure a happy, healthy nation.

Case Study: Water ATMs in Rajasthan

Rajasthan, the desert state of the country, is the largest state in India. With a 10.4% geographical area of the country, it has 5.5% of the country's population and 18.70% of the livestock. But it has only 1.16% of surface water available in the country. During summers, the people in the state face acute water shortage.

We came across an innovate model, run as a Public Private Partnership (PPP), which was used to solve the water problem in the state—Water ATMs. A Scottish energy corporation and the use of modern technology enabled a metamorphosis in two districts of Rajasthan which were earlier infamous for acute water shortage. Through these water ATMs, water is now available 24x7 to the villagers at a cost of Rs 5 for a quantity of 20 litres.

Cairn India, a part of the global natural resources giant Vedanta Group, runs this programme as 'Jeevan Amrit Project'. For this project, Cairn India has collaborated with Public Health Engineering Department (PHED) of the Government of Rajasthan, Tata Projects and the respective village panchayats. The aim of this project is to provide potable drinking water at the doorsteps of the local community. Kiosks with Reverse Osmosis (RO) plants have been installed at several villages such as Guda, Kawas, Jogasar, Bhakharpur, etc. Because of this project, over 22,000 people in the state have benefitted and get potable water to drink. It is expected that the project will be scaled up in the near future to benefit larger sections of the community.

Currently, 22 RO plants (17 with swipe card facilities) cater to the needs of drinking water of the villagers. Villagers get clean drinking water by swiping their cards in the machine just like using a normal bank ATM card to withdraw money.

These cards come with an initial value of Rs 150 and can be further recharged as per their needs by the villagers. Moreover, these machines are also taken to nearby 'Dhanis' (hamlets) at a modest additional cost of Rs 1-2 so that this facility can also be availed of by the people living in surrounding areas. This revenue model helps in making these kiosks self-sustainable. The revenue generated is utilized for operating and maintaining the kiosks in an efficient manner.

The cost of these plants is financed by Cairn India. These plants are installed and delivered by Tata Projects. The Public Health Engineering Department of the Government of Rajasthan (PHED) ensures the provision of a primary water connection and premises to put up the plant. The operation and maintenance of this kiosk is the responsibility of a fifteen-member 'Village Water Committee' formed under the aegis of the panchayat. Dhara, a local NGO, helps in capacity building and handholding the project.

There have been various positive outcomes because of this project. Because of the availability of safe drinking water, there has been a substantial reduction in the occurrence of diseases among children and elderly citizens in these villages. Cases of joint pain among the villagers, which are primarily caused by the high amount of fluoride in drinking water, have also reduced.

Moreover, these projects have also led to the creation of Water Committees which exhibit an efficient model of self-governance. These committees not only undertake the efficient management of the Water ATMs but also assist in various developmental activities in the area.

9

BUILDING THE NEXT-GENERATION HABITATIONS

INCREASING POPULATION AND GROWING CITIES

Between 1 AD and the start of the Industrial Revolution in the early 1800s, human population had grown from approximately 230 million to 1 billion, that is, 0.8% every decade. However, in the next 180 years, it has multiplied to the current 7 billion-plus, which represents a decadal growth of over 11%. In the past century alone, the population quadrupled.

Population growth has been closely accompanied by a simultaneous rise in both wealth creation and extreme poverty. However, there have also been healthcare improvements due to the advancement of life sciences. With the network of global trade routes, fossil fuel-based technologies, industrialization and mechanization, the world income per capita has also grown rapidly, nine times in just the past 150 years. There is a specific aspect to population growth—it is largely concentrated in a few geographical locations. This has led to the emergence of large, very densely populated cities.

For example, in the year 1800, London was the largest city in the world with a population of around 1 million. By 1960, our planet had 111 cities with over a million people. In 2008, this number was a staggering 468.

This concentration of population adds to the pressure on resources at the local level and leads to severe resource scarcities. With increasing wealth and hence increasing per capita energy consumption, the threat of climate change looms large on humanity.

So, modern 'smart cities' have to address the two-pronged challenge of better living standard with reduced emissions and also becoming an economic hub. Also, the 21st century city has to progressively move towards achieving carbon neutrality.

THE CHALLENGE AHEAD

By 2030, India's population is expected to cross the 1.5 billion mark—about 25% more than what it is now. With an almost stagnant Chinese population, by this year India will emerge as the most populous country in the world. By 2030, every fourth global citizen would be an Indian.

Where will these new Indians live? That brings us to the question of how to build the next-generation habitations and be ready to absorb the new population and new aspirations of 2030, which is fairly close. To put things in perspective, in 2000 or so India embarked on its mission to create superhighways and high-speed roads connecting its cities—the Golden Quadrilateral and other state and national highways. Despite a concentrated effort, Indian roads are regarded as woefully inadequate and the country remains the accident capital of the world. The year 2030 is only as far away from us now as today was in 2000.

A widely circulated report by McKinsey predicted that India's GDP would have multiplied by five times by 2030 compared to what it was in 2014.[1] It further claimed that over 70% of new employment would be generated in the cities.[2] How can these cities contribute best to the national growth while also providing a good quality of life to the citizens?

By 2030, it is predicted that sixty-eight Indian cities will have a population of more than a million and a total of 590 million people will live in urban areas—nearly half of the population, as compared

Projected rank in 2030	Current rank in 2014	Country	Projected population in 2030	Population (2010)	% Growth in population between 2015 and 2030
1	2	India	1,523,482,000	1,224,614,000	24.40
2	1	China	1,393,076,000	1,341,335,000	3.90
3	3	USA	361,680,000	310,384,000	16.50
4	4	Indonesia	279,659,000	239,871,000	16.60
5	7	Nigeria	257,815,000	158,423,000	62.70
6	6	Pakistan	234,432,000	173,593,000	35.00
7	5	Brazil	220,492,000	194,946,000	13.10
8	8	Bangladesh	181,863,000	148,692,000	22.30
9	9	Russia	136,429,000	142,958,000	-4.6
10	11	Mexico	135,398,000	113,423,011	19.40

TABLE 1: Population projections for various countries in 2030 and comparison with 2010 population

to the present one-third. What this means is that close to 800 million square metres of commercial and residential space needs to be built annually up to 2030—a new Chicago every year. All this translates to over $1.5–2.5 trillion worth of investment.[3]

That a large portion of India's new growth story will happen in its cities is indisputable. At the same time we also need to figure out how to integrate rural and urban development and ensure that they both help each other grow.

	2011	2001	
	Population (person)	Population (person)	Increase (%)
Mumbai	18,414,288	11,978,595	54
Delhi	16,314,838	9,879,290	65
Kolkata	14,112,536	4,580,513	208
Chennai	8,696,010	4,343,562	100
Bangalore	8,499,399	4,313,266	97
Hyderabad	7,749,334	3,658,477	112
Ahmedabad	6,352,254	4,514,988	41
Pune	5,049,968	2,538,290	99
Surat	4,585,367	2,702,404	70
Jaipur	3,073,750	2,322,395	32
India (overall increase between 2001 and 2011)			15

TABLE 2: Increase in population in Indian cities

A significant challenge facing Indian cities is the issue of extremely and often unmanageably high population densities. Consider Mumbai, which has about 18 million people living in an area of 546 sq. km. Compare that to its Chinese counterpart, Shanghai, which has slightly more, about 22.7 million people, but they live across an area of over 3600 sq. km—about 6.5 times that of

Mumbai. Similarly, the Japanese capital, Tokyo, which also happens
to be the world's largest city, has 37.6 million people living across
an area of 8574 sq. km. Tokyo thus has a population which is about
double that of Mumbai, but an area that is seventeen times larger.
The stress is not exclusive to a particular city, but widely felt across
the nation's metros. Table 2 compares the decadal population
growth rate across some of India's largest cities between 2001 and
2011. Kolkata has almost trebled within the first decade of the 21st
century. Five out of the ten cities listed have grown almost 100% or
more, and all have grown disproportionately higher compared to
the nation's population growth rate of 15.1% for the same period.
The question is—is the growth rate in these cities seen in the first
decade of the 21st century sustainable for the next two decades?
We believe it is not, and hence the need to find new models of
developing Indian cities and habitations.

THE HOUSING ISSUE

One of the biggest issues, economic, social and political, has been
that of providing a house to every citizen. Time and again, the
government, state and centre alike, has embarked on major missions
to provide subsidized housing, even free homes, to millions who
lack proper, all-weather shelter—the largest of such schemes being
the Indira Awas Yojana or IAY, which was started in the mid-1980s.
Till date, over 25 million houses are claimed to have been built
under this aid-for-house scheme in rural areas. The scheme provides
for financial assistance worth Rs 70,000 in the plains and Rs 75,000
in difficult areas (highlands) for construction of houses.[4] Besides
such national schemes, there are a number of state government
schemes for housing. Yet housing remains a challenge.

At the end of 2012, urban India was still short of 18.7 million
houses.[5] Rural India did worse—a shortfall of 43.1 million houses.[6]
It is almost that, in a nation where housing is considered the best
form of financial investment, nearly 62 million households, or 350
million people, need a decent roof above them.

But that is not the real revelation. There is more to the Indian housing contradiction. In 2001, India had a total of 187 million families. In 2011, the total families increased to 247 million, an increase of 60 million families in ten years. While, in 2001, the number of physical houses was 250 million, it went up to 331 million in 2011. Both in 2001 and 2011, the number of physical houses was significantly more than the total families.[7]

Why does this happen? In our view there are three factors for this.

First, housing has become a primary centre for investment and saving. A single family may own many physical houses. This leads to monopolizing of the market—rent escalations which further lead to artificially elevated property prices.

Second, there is significant migration from rural to urban areas— a single family may own a house in a village and another in the city.

Third, because most larger cities have grown in a way that the workplace has become far from home, many house-owners end up buying or renting smaller houses near their workplaces.

Let us now deal with the issue of affordability of houses. By houses we mean decent, low-cost but sturdy houses of about 800 sq. ft each.

Three-quarters of the housing shortage happens for the lowest 30% to 40% of the income group, who cannot afford a house. Let us see what could be an affordable price for a house in this segment.

If we look at figures for monthly per capita expenditure (MPCE) available for the fortieth percentile (which means that 60% of the population will spend more than this and 40% will spend less), with the calculation as shown below, the average affordable price of a house works out to about Rs 455,000 for urban areas and Rs 310,000 for rural areas.

Year	Number of households or families (million)	Number of Physical houses (million)	Excess of physical houses over number of households or families (million)	Actual reported shortage in physical houses (million)
2001	187	250	63	N/A
2011	247	331	84	61.8

TABLE 3: Number of households and actual houses in 2001 and 2011

		Urban	Rural
A	MPCE[8] at fortieth percentile[9]	1757	1075
B	Annual Expenditure per capita (A x 12)	21084	12900
C	Household size[10]	4.5	5
D	Average expenditure of the entire household (B x C)	94,878	64,500
E	Saving Rate (Excess of income over expenditure)	20%	20%
F	Approximate income per household at 40th percentile of MPCE	113,853	77,400
G	Times of annual income which can be invested in a house	4	4
H	Possible house that a given household at 40th percentile can afford (F x G)	455,414	309,600

TABLE 4: Calculating the threshold of affordable housing for India—assuming no government support

Compared to this, what is the cost of construction of a decent house? Assuming no cost for land, it comes to about Rs 360,000. Thus 60% of Indians can afford to own a house at their own expense, provided they are given land at low rates.

For the remaining 40% of the population, there has to be a graded financial support system which increases as one goes down the MPCE percentile. Thus, if the market is rectified, housing is not an impossible challenge—and with limited support from the government the dream of a decent house for all can be realized.

How do we set a vision for these upcoming areas into habitations and cities? How will such cities integrate with the rural areas and how will they blend with the overall objective of a smart habitation? These will be the challenges to look at next.[11]

What would be the characteristics of a smart city?

1. Smart habitations have to be based on the value they bring to national economic objectives.

Component	% to total cost	Rs/sq.ft.	Rs thousand	Remarks
Cement	10-15%	70	56	300-350 Bags
Steel	8-10%	40	32	2-3 kg/sq. ft. @ Rs 16/kg
Other Material	25-30%	100	80	Sand, bricks, aggregates
Labor	25-30%	120	96	Mason, contractor and workers
Finishing	20-25%	120	96	Doors, windows, furniture, electrical, plumbing, decoration etc.
Total	100%	450	360	

TABLE 5: Cost of construction of a house—not accounting for cost of land

2. Smart habitations preserve and protect local culture and help bridge different segments of society.
3. Smart habitations are areas of equal opportunities for all segments of society. They provide enterprise an environment for new ideas and create original research for application in products and services.
4. Smart habitations provide quality infrastructure, healthcare and education to all.
5. Smart habitations are zones of environment protection that generate clean energy and reduce, recycle and reuse waste.
6. Smart habitations are a reflection of human diversity, different regions and even nations—they are zones of biodiversity and celebrate their multiplicity.
7. Smart habitations are based on effective and cost-efficient usage of information technology and communication systems for smart governance and smart citizenship. They also promote electronic monetary transactions.
8. Smart habitations provide equal justice to all and dignity to all economic classes—treating all labour and professionals with respect.
9. Smart habitations coexist with nearby rural areas and bring value addition to the people there.
10. Smart habitations are clean, transparent, well governed, have zero corruption and emanate happiness to the residents and visitors alike.

Any discussion of planning must include the empowerment of rural regions, which is critically important from the perspective of inclusive development, sustained peace and shared prosperity. The untapped potential of our villages is a great treasure. Can smart habitation planning also consider this as a goal?

We visited Canada for a week in September 2010. We went to Vancouver in British Columbia where there was a meeting with premier Gordon Campbell. He proudly announced that he was going to make Vancouver a carbon neutral city by 2015, and then make the entire state of British Columbia carbon neutral too.

Carbon Emission and Carbon Neutrality

Carbon dioxide emissions into the atmosphere, and the emissions of other GHGs, are often associated with the burning of fossil fuels, like natural gas, crude oil and coal. For instance, every litre of petrol burnt yields 2.3 kg of carbon dioxide.

Carbon neutrality means a particular city or area is not generating any extra carbon dioxide emission. It can be achieved both by reducing emission—such as use of solar power, electric cars and other non-polluting systems, and planting trees as they absorb carbon dioxide from the atmosphere.

In February 2010, during a meeting in Maldives, the president of the island country told us about the nation's mission of becoming carbon neutral, the first to achieve the status amongst all the countries in the world. These are indeed promising trends in the world.

THE CASE OF 100 SMART CITIES MISSION

In 2014, as a new government took over in Delhi, the prime minister declared the mission of creating 100 smart cities. A commitment was also made for the rejuvenation of 500 other cities with a population of 1 lakh and above. While figures vary, it will entail an estimated cost of more than Rs 40 lakh crore over ten to fifteen years across the nation—based on better technology, superior management and modern governance.

The planning of the smart cities has to keep in mind two important aspects. One is to provide a livable quality infrastructure with clean and green environment as used to exist in the past. The second is to establish environment-friendly industries which provide value-added employment to 60% of the globally skilled youth living in the 100 smart cities and nearby villages.

Thus, these 100 smart cities could be a hub for clean green manufacturing industries that feature in the twenty-one sectors listed in the 'Make in India' programme. Each smart city should become a hub for hosting at least three to four big industries which cater to the global market.

Setting up a smart city requires land, say 2500 acres for each smart city, as the core economic engine. It makes sense to make the farmers giving this land partners in this SPV project, since land is a primary and basic fundamental component for building smart cities. To take care of the farmer's long-term interests, 50% of the land can be valued at four times of the market price for their alternate livelihood and rest of the 50% of the land value can be taken as an investment cost for the Special Purpose Vehicle (SPV) formed for each smart city.

We have a working model operating in Pune, Maharashtra, called 'Magarpatta Cooperative Society' where all the farmers joined together and invested their land as a primary investment and raised bank funding to create a beautiful clean and green smart city. Today the farmers are part owners of the enterprise.

Hence, the government can consider and make an amendment to the land acquisition bill to make farmers partners while acquiring the land for a business proposition such as a smart city. Once this is done the overall development cost also comes down.

BEYOND SMART: CITIES OF WISDOM AND HAPPINESS[12]

A city is a habitable area physically demarcated by geographical boundaries. It has a population demography, infrastructure, civic amenities, governance, judicial systems and political system. These are the physical components of a city. There is, however, another component of a city which is purely subjective. It pertains to the cultural, social and ethical values of the city, the temperament of its people and their relationship with each other, in a sense the soul of the city.

Today, cities are characterized by booming population density, with millions of humans literally stacked on top of each other—in vertical spanning structures. Cities, especially in Asia, can pack up to 50,000 people in a single square kilometre. A single building, such as the World Trade Centre, can be the working space for over 50,000 professionals. Much of the urban lifestyle is about reaching office, school or business on time after weaving through congested traffic, and living and working in cocooned air-conditioned environments.

Uneven pricing and unplanned zoning have led to homes being far away from work, and sometimes even farther away from commercial and entertainment centres.

A resident of Mumbai, on an average, takes 95 minutes to travel back and forth between home and office—about 10% of the total time awake is hence spent on the road. The number is not different from one megacity to another. *The Economist*, in a 2011 research, had discovered that commuting time is one of the primary reasons for unhappiness among urban professionals. In most of the developing world, rising rent rates, soaring pollution, job stress, falling health standards coupled with the constant struggle for clean water and reliable supply of electricity are sources of tension. The truth is, cities are reducing their citizens to emotionally rudderless entities, with little to observe and admire, and becoming a breeding ground for four concerns—mistrust, fear, anxiety and aversion.

How to address these concerns is the key question in designing modern cities. How do we convert despair to hope, fear to belief, anxiety to ease and aversion to compassion and love are the soft measures that need to be a part of urban planning. This is what we term as 'city with soul'—a city which offers not just amenities, but also happiness; not just economics, but also values.

City	Average commute time back and forth from office to home
Mumbai	95 minutes
Delhi	87
Bangalore	80
New York	63

TABLE 6: Average commute time in major cities

There is a difference between measuring a city's happiness and its prosperity. While a fast-paced city like Bangalore would have a higher income level for its working population, the problems of high cost of living, congestion, traffic problems and long travelling distances would undermine the positives of the city. Further, the crime and accident rate and socio-economic disparities are of more concern to the city's population than the industrial and economic prosperity of the city. These are the reasons why a person might like to work in a city, but not prefer to live in it.

A city's well-being thus can also be defined by a happiness index. Bhutan, for instance, has prepared a Gross Happiness Index (GHI) comprising socio-economic factors such as psychological well-being, standard of living, good governance, health, education, community vitality, cultural and ecological diversity.

EPILOGUE

It was a cool autumn evening, a rather breezy one. The sun had just set, leaving the moon and its starry friends. On the shores of Kerala stood Veera the Buffalo, tethered to her place outside the house of owner, Jagir. Nearby were a dozen cows, which too Jagir owned, that were busy chatting to each other. After a day filled with work, Veera gazed into the shimmering water, wondering what it was that made the Arabian Sea shimmer. She had overheard Jagir telling someone it was a substance called thorium which was present in the waters off Kerala, and that it carried a lot of energy! As Veera looked towards the sea, she heard a faint noise in the skies. She looked up and saw a flying object, much smaller than a plane but without any pilot in it. She wondered whether it was an alien space ship.

Suddenly, there was a lightning flash in the sky. It simultaneously lit up the thorium, the flying object and Veera in its light. For some strange reason, the three forms became connected and they started a conversation.

Veera: Hey, you flying object! Are you an alien?

Unknown flying object: . . . Beep . . . Beep . . . *(pause, followed by a very slow mechanical voice)* I am an Unmanned Aerial Vehicle called UAV. There are only three of my kind—used for experiments by the armed forces, but since I am never assigned any work I am just looking around.

Veera: Oh! So you are UAV? What is your name?

UAV: Yes. They call me Teja.

*(Thorium, which was shimmering in the ocean,
then spoke. Its voice was deep.)*

Thorium: I cannot believe we are all talking! My name is Thor. I am Thorium. I am all over these waters.

Veera was surprised at the conversation.

Veera: I am a buffalo called Veera. I belong to a farmer called Jagir.

Teja (UAV): How are you, Veera? Why are you standing away from the others?

Veera: That is because I am sad. I do my best, better than the rest of my colleagues out there, and yet I am laughed at. I am considered stupid.

Thor: But why? I heard you animals are doing great service to humans!

Veera: Yes. You see, we the buffaloes of India produce 55% of the total milk in the nation. Out of the 170 million buffaloes in the world, 111 million live in India. That is two of every three buffaloes in the world lives in India.

Thor: Hmmm . . .

Veera: We provide a core advantage to India's agriculture. Since we are not present in such large number in the rest of the world, no other nation will do any research to ease our pains or increase our productivity. But even India devotes very little effort to our betterment. Nobody recognizes it. I am so neglected. I am sad.

*This line struck a chord with Thor, who rose up
from deep contemplation.*

Thor: My dear Veera! I can totally understand your feeling, as we are going through a similar treatment. Look at my kind. Look at us, spread out in the sea. We are all over these shores. And we are filled with energy.

Teja: Really?

Thor: Yes. In fact, 62 kg of thorium can generate the same energy as 500 kg of uranium or 10,000,000 kg of coal. Everybody talks of coal and uranium, but I am ignored.

Veera: How is that?

Thor: You will be surprised to know that just like you I am abundant, and almost exclusive to India. India has the largest reserves of thorium in the world, with over 650,000 tonnes. This is more than one-fourth of the total deposits of thorium; comparatively we have barely 1% of the world uranium deposits.

*Teja came lower to have a better look at Thor,
then asked a question . . .*

Teja: What about the energy you can generate?

Thor: It is believed that the amount of energy in thorium reserves on earth is more than the combined total energy in remaining petroleum, coal, other fossil fuels and uranium. India is an energy-shortage country and yet I am lying here untapped with the potential to make India the largest energy generator in the world, that too without any of the pollution which coal causes. I am India's energy advantage.

Teja: Oh, Thor. I can see your pain and tragedy. I have a similar experience.

*Veera listened to Teja carefully. She could not believe she had
met two others with a similar story.*

Veera: How? What is your story, Teja?

Teja: You see friends! I am an Unmanned Aerial Vehicle. I can fly to great distances, reach faraway places at great speeds. I do not need a pilot too.

Thor: How can you fly without a human pilot?

Teja: Thor! I have computers and signalling and communication system. While I can do a lot of flying all by myself, I can also be controlled by a remote pilot sitting somewhere in a room in full safety. Imagine the safety that provides. The Indian Air Force spends more than $2.5 million to train every pilot who takes control of an expensive aircraft. Dozens of these aircraft have crashed, resulting in pilot casualties. That too when we were not even in a situation of war! Every time an accident happens, the life of a human is at risk. I eliminate this risk by not carrying any pilot inside. I can perform surveillance, combat enemies both on the ground and in the sky and even if I crash no human life is at risk. I am the future of defence. Moreover, I am easier to build, cheaper to manufacture and can easily be produced within India.

Veera was astonished to hear this.

Veera: Oh! I overheard Jagir reading from the newspaper about India buying jets from abroad! What about that?

Thor: Yes! I heard that too.

Teja: Yes, India is acquiring several fighter jets from France. The latest ones are called Rafale and each of these will cost about $200 million dollars, or about Rs 1200 crore. The deal has been in process for about three or four years and two separate governments have been pursuing and negotiating for it. But imagine this! The best-known version of my kind, a UAV called Predator, costs about $4 million or Rs 24 crore per unit. That means for the price of one Rafale, we could have made 50 UAVs. These UAVs are being used in Afghanistan, Pakistan and Iraq by the Americans. I am not saying we should not buy jets, but in the future, wars will be fought against soft targets, as in the case of terrorism, and I can carry weapons in my arsenal. But nobody cares about me too. I am just a test version, and I am afraid no defence force will recommend me as I don't need a pilot and I will be scrapped soon. I am a potential future advantage of India, but I am deserted too.

Thor, Teja and Veera then said together:

We are the untapped advantages of India. One of us can create revolution in India's agriculture. Other can make India energy surplus without causing pollution. And the third can provide defence capability of global standard to suit our needs at an economical cost. India needs to focus on us and many other hidden advantages which can lead the country to guaranteed health, education, security and a decent standard of living.

When we thought up the idea of a candid discussion by respected Buffalo, most respected Thorium and beloved UAV, we realized that the imagination has tremendous potential to make the youth of the nation and its thinkers and doers realize that the mission is achievable. I have the unique experience of meeting about 21 million youth of my country in the last two decades. I met these youth in thousands of meetings across all parts of the country. At question time, there was always a request: 'Give us the message.' I gave my message in the form of an eleven-point oath on what the youth can do and also a slogan, I can do it, We can do it, India will do it.

AFTERWORD

ADDRESS AND INTERACTION WITH THE PARTICIPANTS OF CREATING A LIVEABLE EARTH

SESSION I, IIM SHILLONG

HOW TO MAKE OUR PLANET MORE LIVEABLE?

'The sustainable development enables the realization of green, clean environment without pollution, having prosperity without poverty, peace without fear of war and a happy place to live for all citizens everywhere in the world.'

On 27 July 2015, Dr A.P.J. Abdul Kalam was in Shillong to deliver a series of lectures at the IIM there. The subject was Creating a Liveable Earth, the title of a short course for students there. He hoped, in the first lecture he had written for the occasion, that his presentation and their responses could take the 'shape of an action plan for the course participants in various sustainable development systems which could preserve and nurture the planet and its people':

'While doing these assignments, I am sure all of you would have realized what an interconnected world we all live in and how the future is a function of our actions today. I will be focusing now on exploring these connections, ideas and challenges. Our journey begins today where we will analyse new avenues of global prosperity and peace, the creative leadership needed for such a change and also the all-important aspect of how to preserve and enhance our environment while all this happens.'

As he put it, 'the planet's biggest problem today is to do with sustainability, environmental decline, global poverty, disease, conflict and many other sideshows that go on around them. These are all interconnected—it is one big problem, which is that the way we are doing things cannot go on. Sustainable development is an organizing principle for human life on a finite planet. It suggests a desirable future state for human societies in which living conditions and resource-use meet human needs without undermining the sustainability of natural systems and the environment, so that future generations may also have their needs met.'

He pointed out, 86% of the total energy produced comes from fossil fuel; around 14% comes from renewable energy and the nuclear sector. In this situation, it is essential to find innovative methods to reduce the consumption of power from fossil fuels and increase the deployment of renewable energy systems.

In his usual way, he offered specific alternatives to the problems. 'India has 900 million mobile users, and 250,000 cellphone towers, which consume nearly 2 billion litres of diesel for power. If we convert these installations into solar-powered systems, we save about $1.7 billion and offset 5 million tonnes of CO_2 emission and gain carbon credit. Next, if we transform all our 600,000 villages where 700 million people live and equip them with solar-powered homes and street lights, we may offset around 60% of fossil fuel usage in that sector . . .'

WHAT CONNECTS THE WORLD?

What are the fundamental parameters which connect nations on one unified platform, what tools enable such connectivity and what specific agendas are needed to bring the world together, he asked. He included the environment, trade and economics, security, health and education among these. These elements connect the world with a compounding positive effect, he said, meaning that the well-being of one nation on these parameters implies the well-being of every other nation as well.

'The environment, for instance, has become an issue of international importance that affects health, habitation and crop patterns across the globe. We have now reached the farthest places in the solar system, looking into Pluto, but we are yet to secure a future for our home planet.'

In essence he suggested it was time ways were found to live in peace and prosperity as a global community in a clean world.

In his World Vision 2030: Liveable Planet Earth, he wondered what was the unique vision that would replace military superiority between nations. 'I have a feeling that we need a great vision, higher than individuals, ideologies, party affiliation, political ambitions and the present technological superiority. Dear friends, can we visualize what it should be?'

We needed to leave a sustainable world where we had taken less from nature than what we had given to it. As long as there were inequities of development between urban and rural areas; between neighbourhoods; in sharing valuable resources, peace would elude us. Particularly, modern technology has made the world a global village. Hence tolerance for inequities would also come down.

He had prepared a distinctive profile for the world's nations in 2030:

1. A world where the divide between rural and urban, rich and poor, developed and developing has narrowed down.
2. A world where there is an equitable distribution of and adequate access to energy and quality water.
3. A world where the core competencies of each nation are identified. Missions synergizing the core competencies of different nations lead to economic advantage and faster development for all the societies.
4. A world where all the students of all societies are imparted education with value system.

5. A world where affordable quality health care is available to all.

6. A world where the governance is responsive, transparent and corruption-free.

7. A world where crime against women and children is absent and none in the society feels alienated.

8. A world in which every nation is able to give a clean, green environment to all its citizens.

9. A world that is prosperous, healthy, secure, devoid of terrorism, peaceful and happy and follows a sustainable growth path.

10. A world with creative leadership, which ensures effective mechanisms to resolve conflicts between nations and societies in a timely manner keeping overall peace and prosperity of the world as a goal.

His suggestion to evolve a vision which will unify nations and work for the sustainability of the earth and humanity included a World Knowledge Platform for Global Action. This could emerge as a 'network of universities, government agencies and industries for participation of policy makers, students, academia and entrepreneurs. It should focus on identifying global problems, researching solutions in a multinational manner, and delivering through local cooperation and enterprise-based approach in the long term for sustainability. It needs to be funded as an international cooperative venture with about $4 billion over the next five years with dedicated spending to developing customizable and scalable solutions . . .'

Among the threats such a platform could identify were global environment degradation and climate change. Another was the threat of trade deficit and global economic recession, which is affecting many nations, including India. The third threat was poverty. In spite of all the growth, 3 billion people of the world needed improvement in the quality of their life.

One way of solving problems was youth dynamics, the greatest opportunity available to the world, since the power of youth was the most powerful resource on earth, he concluded. Sadly, the lecture was not completed, and these and many other programmes he had worked so intensively on were left on the path to fulfilment . . .

Righteousness in the heart

Where there is righteousness in the heart
There is beauty in the character.
When there is beauty in the character,
There is harmony in the home.
When there is harmony in the home.
There is an order in the nation.
When there is order in the nation,
There is peace in the world.

NOTES

2. FROM FALLEN HERO TO RISING STAR

1. Rakesh Krishnan Simha, 'Remembering India's Forgotten Holocaust,' *Tehelka*, http://www.tehelka.com/2014/06/remembering-indias-forgotten-holocaust/
2. Shashi Tharoor, 'The Ugly Briton,' http://content.time.com/time/magazine/article/ 0,9171,2031992,00.html
3. Dennis Merrill, *Bread and Ballot: The United States and India's Economic Development* (North Carolina: University of North Carolina Press, 2010).
4. Lester Brown, 'US-India: Dealing With Monsoon Failure,' http://www.theglobalist.com/us-india-dealing-with-monsoon-failure/
5. Ibid.
6. '67 Years after Independence, Indian farmers have disappeared from the economic radar screen,' http://devinder-sharma.blogspot.in/2014/08/67-years-after- independence-indian.html
7. Ibid.
8. Inder Malhotra, 'Swallowing the Humiliation,' *Indian Express*, 12 July 2010, http://archive.indianexpress.com/news/swallowing-the-humiliation/ 645168/0
9. In PPP terms.
10. Drawn from Jawaharlal Nehru's speech to the Indian Constituent Assembly in 1947.
11. Daron Acemoglu and James A. Robinson, *Why Nations Fail: The Origins of Power, Prosperity and Poverty* (London: Profile Books, 2013).
12. Ibid.
13. Former Singaporean President Devan Nair, who was exiled to Canada,

went on to state that Lee's methods of suing his opponents into bankruptcy was a misuse of political powers. In response, Lee sued Nair in Canada.

14. Rukmini S., '16th Lok Sabha will be richest, have most MPs with criminal charges,' *Hindu*, http://www.thehindu.com/news/national/16th-lok-sabha-will-berichesthave-most-mps-with-criminal-charges/article6022513.ece

15. Ibid.

16. https://www.bcgperspectives.com/content/articles financial_institutions_corporate_strategy_portfolio_management_global_wealth_2012_battle_regain_strength/?chapter=2#chapter2_section4

17. Forbes' list of billionaires.

18. World Factbook, CIA website.

3. PATHWAYS TO NATIONAL PRODUCTIVITY

1. Taken from public data available on Wikipedia, http://en.wikipedia.org/wiki/Telecommunications_statistics_in_India

2. Akhilesh Tilotia, *The Making of India: Gamechanging Transitions* (New Delhi: Rupa Publications, 2015).

3. Government of India data, https://data.gov.in/catalog/production-imports-and-consumptionfertilizers#web_catalog_tabs_block_10

4. The Cola model is universal, unlike Agni and BrahMos, as will be evident later.

5. http://en.wikipedia.org/wiki/American_Civil_War

6. Based on the company's annual report and data from the World Bank.

7. M. Rochan, 'Rising Wages May Erode China's Low-Cost Manufacturing Advantage,' 6 January 2014, http://www.ibtimes.co.uk/rising-wages-may-erode-chinas-low-cost-manufacturing-advantage-1431142

8. Ibid.

9. 'The Boomerang Effect,' *Economist*, 21 April 2012, http://www.economist.com/node/21552898

10. Michael E. Porter, 'The Competitive Advantage of Nations,' *Harvard Business Review*, https://hbr.org/1990/03/the-competitive-advantage-of-nations

11. Ibid.

4. BUILDING THE HUMAN RESOURCE

1. National Skill Development Policy 2009.
2. Nishant Arya, 'Can India harness its demographic dividend?' *Financial Express*, 4 January 2015, http://www.financialexpress.com/article/economy/can-india-harness-itsdemographic-dividend/26034/
3. Rajeev Mantri and Harsh Gupta, 'The Conclusive Case for School Choice,' *Mint*, 22 October 2013, http://www.livemint.com/Opinion/LI8HU3WD2LsgNO8lPVyhgK/The-conclusive-case-for-school-choice.html
4. David Russell Schilling, 'Knowledge Doubling Every 12 Months, Soon to be Every 12 Hours,' 19 April 2013, http://www.industrytap.com/knowledge-doubling-every-12-months-soon-to-be-every-12-hours/3950
5. Liz Wiseman, *Rookie Smarts: Why Learning Beats Knowing in the New Game of Work* (London: Harper Business, 2014).
6. Ibid.
7. Ibid.
8. Taken from World Intellectual Property Organization (WIPO), http://www.wipo.int/portal/en/index.html
9. Ibid
10. Richard L. Burleson, 'How the Shale Boom Saved a US Economy That Was on the Brink,' 18 August 2014, http://www.burlesonllp.com/?t=40&an=32127&format=xml
11. Now in Pakistan
12. 'A Tribute to Hinduism, Education in Ancient Times,' http://www.hinduwisdom.info/Education_in_Ancient_India.htm

5. ENSURING A HEALTHY NATION FOR ALL

1. Based on 2006 data.
2. 'India's Record since Independence,' *Wall Street Journal*, 15 August 2013, http://blogs.wsj.com/indiarealtime/2013/08/15/indiasrecord-since-independence/
3. Amartya Sen and Jean Dreze, *An Uncertain Glory: India and Its Contradictions* (London: Penguin Books, 2014).
4. S. Sreevidyaa and B.W.C. Sathiyasekaran, 'High caesarean rates in Madras (India): A population-based cross sectional study (2003).'

5. D.P. Agrawal and Pankaj Goyal, 'Hospitals in Ancient India,' http://www.indianscience.org/essays/21-%20E—Hospitals%20in%20India%20in%20ancient%20period%20and%20medieval%20period.pdf

6. In this analysis only countries with a population of over 2 million have been considered.

7. 'A Healthy Population is a Fundamental Ingredient of Inclusive Development and Nation building—Vice President of India (2013),' http://pib.nic.in/newsite/mbErel.aspx?relid=97059

8. 'Economic loss due to deaths in India to increase to 5% of GDP,' 18 March 2013, http://www.biospectrumindia.com/biospecindia/news/185477/economicloss-deaths-india-increase-gdp

9. 'Scientists warn of rise in diseases spread from animals to humans,' *Telegraph*, 4 January 2010, http://www.telegraph.co.uk/news/health/news/6930130/Scientists-warn-of-rise-in-diseases-spreadfrom-animals-to-humans.html

10. Ibid

11. Moby and Miyun Park, ed., *Gristle: From Factory Farms to Food Safety* (New York: The New Press, 2010).

12. Ibid.

13. Michael Greger, 'The Human/Animal Interface: Emergence and Resurgence of Zoonotic Infectious Diseases, Humane Society Institute for Science and Policy (2005).'

14. Bostwana (23.4%), Lesotho (23.3%), Swaziland (26%), South Africa (17.3%)

15. 'Protecting Our Food System from Current and Emerging Animal and Plant Diseases and Pathogens: Implications for Research, Education, Extension, and Economics,' NAREEE Advisory Board Meeting and Focus Session, Washington, DC, 27-29 October 2004.

16. F.A. Murphy, 'Emerging zoonoses,' *Emerging Infectious Diseases* 4(3): 429-35.

17. Broad Institute data, http://www.broadinstitute.org/annotation/genome/mycobacterium_tuberculosis_spp/Info.html

18. http://www.allaboutheaven.org/overload/139/124/measles

19. Data from the World Health Organization.

20. Ibid.

21. I-poshan stands for Intelligent Poshan. Poshan is the Hindi word for nutrition.

22. Amartya Sen and Jean Dreze, *An Uncertain Glory: India and Its Contradictions* (London: Penguin Books, 2014).

6. A DIGITALLY EMPOWERED INDIA

1. Bianca Vazquez Toness and Bibhudatta Pradhan, 'India on Cusp of "Digital Revolution", Minister Says,' Bloomberg Business, 29 October 2014, http://www.bloomberg.com/news/articles/2014-10-29/india-on-cusp-of-digital-revolution-minister-says
2. Ibid.
3. 'Internet Users by Country (Year 2014),' http://www.internetlivestats.com/internet-usersby-country/
4. Shrutika Verma, 'India to have 213 million mobile Internet users by June: Iamai IMRB Report,' *Mint*, 13 January 2015, http://www.livemint.com/Politics/RPQoGQAAhIP8ZwmECrChpK/India-to-have-213-million-mobile-Internet-users-by-June-Rep.html
5. Harsimran Julka and Apurva Vishwanath, 'Matrimony portals making serious efforts to counter rising tide of divorces, ensure lasting unions,' *Economic Times*, 26 June 2013, http://articles.economictimes.indiatimes.com/2013-06-26/news/40206906_1_portals-online-bharatmatrimony-com
6. Srijan runs a technology for a base of the pyramid organization called 3 Billion Initiative based out of Ahmedabad and builds affordable mobile-based solutions.
7. Malini Bhupta, 'India set to become world's fastest growing e-commerce market,' *Business Standard*, 6 February 2015, http://www.business-standard.com/article/companies/india-set-tobecome-world-s-fastest-growing-e-commerce-market-115020601227_1.html
8. Ibid.
9. Anirban Sen, 'IT sector exports to grow 13-15% in FY15, says Nasscom,' *Mint*, 11 February 2014, http://www.livemint.com/Industry/BrMXBnGtlewsRoN99KqKCM/ITsector-exports-to-grow-1315-in-FY15-Nasscom.html
10. Anupama Airy and Gaurav Choudhury, 'Oil price slide set to bring down subsidy bill,' *Hindustan Times*, 20 January 2015, http://www.hindustantimes.com/business-news/oil-price-slide-setto-bring-down-subsidy-bill/article1-1309417.aspx

11. '2.97 million professionals employed in IT/ITeS sector in FY13: Government,' *Economic Times*, 3 May 2013, http://articles. economictimes.indiatimes.com/2013-05-03/news/39009441_1_rs-4-11-lakh-crore-it-ites-exports-professionals

12. 'IT & ITeS Industry in India,' India Brand Equity Foundation, October 2014, updated February 2015, http://www.ibef.org/industry/information-technology-india.aspx

13. 'Physicians (per 1,000 people),' The World Bank, http://data.worldbank.org/indicator/SH.MED.PHYS.ZS

14. 'Hospital beds (per 1,000 people),' The World Bank, http://data.worldbank.org/indicator/SH.MED.BEDS.ZS

15. http://en.wikipedia.org/wiki/Share_My_Lesson and http://www.sharemylesson.com/

16. IIN stands for Idea Internet Network. Idea is a major cellular phone network operator in India.

17. 'India's first ever dedicated navigation satellite launched,' *Daily News and Analysis*, 2 July 2013, http://www.dnaindia.com/scitech/report-indias-first-ever-dedicated-navigation-satellite-launched-1855830

18. 'US Military GPS, United States of America,' http://www.army-technology.com/projects/gps-block-iif-satellites/gps-block-iif-satellites5.html

19. Jayshree P. Upadhyay, 'Only 28% of Jan Dhan Yojana accounts active,' *Business Standard*, 22 January 2015, http://www.business-standard.com/article/finance/sbi-yes-bank-lead-in-zerobalance-accounts-under-jan-dhan-yojana-115012100174_1.html

20. 'Not All "Bank Accounts" in India Are Active: World Bank,' https://www.thedollarbusiness.com/not-all-bank-accounts-in-india-are-activeworld-bank/

21. Akhilesh Tilotia, *The Making of India: Gamechanging Transitions* (New Delhi: Rupa Publications, 2015).

22. Prabhakar Sinha and Namrata Singh, 'India loses Rs 10 lakh crore from black economy every year,' *Economic Times*, 22 March 2010.

23. Ibid.

24. Appu Esthose Suresh and Dinesh Unnikrishnan, 'Govt report says 4 in every 1,000 notes are fake,' *Mint*, 8 August 2011, http://www.livemint.com/Home-Page/9NSxNFvWkjsNYOfmkHeCWM/Govt-report-says-4-in-every-1000-notes-are-fake.html

25. Report on Indian Retail by KPMG, 2014.

26. Ibid.

27. Liana B. Baker, Jessica Toonkel and Ryan Vlastelica, 'Alibaba surges 38 percent on massive demand in market debut,' 19 September 2014, http://www.reuters.com/article/2014/09/19/us-alibaba-ipo-idUSKBN0HD2CO20140919

28. 'Alibaba: The world's greatest bazaar,' *Economist*, 20 March 2013, http://www.economist.com/news/briefing/21573980-alibaba-trailblazing-chinese-internet-giant-will-soon-gopublic-worlds-greatest-bazaar

29. Ibid.

30. Tom Lasseter, 'India's Stagnant Courts Resist Reform,' Bloomberg Business, 8 January 2015, http://www.bloomberg.com/news/articles/2015-01-08/indias-courts-resistreform-backlog-at-314-million-cases

31. Ibid.

7. CREATING A 21st CENTURY POLITICAL SYSTEM AND GOVERNANCE OF ETHICS AND EFFICIENCY

1. The list is in descending order of clean administration.

2. NOTA is the acronym for 'None of the Above'.

3. Mussoorie is a hill station in Uttarakhand. The Lal Bahadur Shastri Academy for Administration is one of the premier training and orientation institutions for civil service professionals in India.

8. WATER EQUATIONS AND THE RIGHT TO WATER FOR ALL

1. http://thewaterproject.org/water_stats

2. 'Diarrhoea: Why children are still dying and what can be done,' 2009, http://www.unicef.org/health/index_51412.html.

3. 'Executive Summary of "Costs and benefits of water and sanitation improvements at the global level",' World Health Organization, www.who.int/water_sanitation_health/wsh0404summary/en/

4. http://infochangeindia.org/agenda/the-politics-of-water/2015-334-million-indians-will-still-lack-access-to-safe-water-supply.html

5. http://water.org/country/india/

6. http://water.worldbank.org/news/inadequate-sanitation-costs-indiaequivalent-64-percent-gdp

7. http://www.thethirdpole.net/indias-groundwater-drops-to-criticallevels/
8. http://timesofindia.indiatimes.com/city/ahmedabad/Groundwater levels-in-Ahmedabad-take-another-deep-plunge/articleshow/10912228.cms
9. http://www.cess.ac.in/cesshome/wp%5CWater.pdf
10. Adapted from http://www.ais.unwater.org/ais/pluginfile.php/356/mod_page/content/111/CountryReport_India.pdf

9. BUILDING THE NEXT-GENERATION HABITATIONS

1. McKinsey Report on Urbanization (2010).
2. Ibid.
3. G.R.K. Reddy and Srijan Pal Singh, *Smart and Human: Building Cities of Wisdom* (New Delhi: HarperCollins Publishers India, 2015).
4. http://203.122.36.41:8080/iimsdatafiles/IIMSData/UploadFile/87_2126_Indira%20Awaas%20Yojana.pdf
5. 'Urban housing shortage declines 25% in five years to 18.7 mn in 2012,' *Business Standard*, 23 September 2012, http://www.businessstandard.com/article/economy-policy/urban-housing-shortagedeclines-25-in-five-years-to-18-7-mn-in-2012-112092302010_1.html
6. Arjun Kumar, 'Estimating Rural Housing Shortage,' *Economic and Political Weekly*, http://www.epw.in/review-rural-affairs/estimating-rural-housing-shortage.html
7. '1.2 crore vacant homes—This one number tells us all that is wrong with Indian real estate,' http://www.firstpost.com/business/1-2-crore-vacant-homes-one-number-tells-us-wrong-indian-real-estate-2220612.html
8. At MMRP or modified mixed reference period.
9. http://mospi.nic.in/mospi_new/upload/press-release-68th-HCE.pdf, page 4.
10. 'Average size of rural households declines,' *Business Standard*, April 2005, http://www.business-standard.com/article/economy-policy/average-size-of-rural-households-declines-105040601086_1.html
11. This section is adapted from G.R.K. Reddy and Srijan Pal Singh, *Smart and Human: Building Cities of Wisdom* (New Delhi: HarperCollins Publishers India, 2015).
12. Ibid.

INDEX